The Poet's Other Voice

The Poet's Other Voice

Conversations on Literary

Translation / Edwin Honig

The University of Massachusetts Press

Amherst, 1985

Printed in the United States of America

Library of Congress Cataloging in Publication Data

Honig, Edwin.

The poet's other voice.

Includes bibliographies.

1. Poetry—Translating. I. Title.

PN1059.T7H66   1985   418'.02   84–28066

ISBN 0–87023–476–5

ISBN 0–87023–477–3 (pbk.)

Earlier versions of these conversations appeared as follows:

"Conversations with Translators, I," *MLN* 90, no. 6 (1975): 896–912 (John Hollander);
913–20 (Herbert Mason).

"Conversations with Translators, II," *MLN* 91, no. 5 (1976): 1073–83 (Octavio Paz);
1084–98 (Richard Wilbur).

"Conversations with Translators, III," *MLN* 91, no. 6 (1976): 1572–87 (Robert Fitzgerald);
1588–1602 (Christopher Middleton).

" 'Just Bring Me Back Alive': Translation as Adam's Dream" [with Ben Belitt], *Modern Poetry Studies* 7, no. 2 (1976): 88–104.

"Conversations with Two Translators by Edwin Honig," *Poetry Society of America Bulletin* 70 (Spring 1980): 16–24 (Michael Hamburger); 25–35 (Edmund Keeley).

"A Conversation about Translation between Edwin Honig and John Hayward in Jerusalem on March 21, 1977," *Poetry Society of America Bulletin* 71 (Winter 1981): 29–33.

"A Conversation on Translation between Edwin Honig and Willard Trask," *Poetry Society of America Bulletin* 72 (Winter 1982): 17–22.

The author is grateful to the National Endowment for the Humanities for a Senior Fellowship grant which made possible the investigation of the project on which this book is based.

To the memory of
ROBERT FITZGERALD (1910–1985),
WILLARD TRASK (1900–1980),
and
MAX HAYWARD (1925–1979)

I do think the poet's growth comes through encounters with the alien, the foreign, the strange, and the unknown. And one of the simplest and most creative ways of considering the act of translation is to regard it as a minimal, perhaps vestigial, but still exemplary encounter with the other.

CHRISTOPHER MIDDLETON

The history of the different civilizations is the history of their translations. Each civilization, as each soul, is different, unique. Translation is our way to face this otherness of the universe and history.

OCTAVIO PAZ

Contents

Preface

In the mid-seventies, a symposium on poetic translation was conceived at Brown University. It was to have been a three-day public affair and the participants were to be poets and writers distinguished for their long practice and commitment to the art of translation. When funding for the project proved inadequate, the hope for some public interchange as a vivid in-the-flesh occasion fell through. Any semblance of the idea might have vanished had not a grant from the National Endowment for the Humanities become available, enabling me to readapt the original possibility by seeking out many of the same persons privately. I would go to where each lived, and there instigate unrehearsed conversations on translation. Whatever special news I might pick up would be conveyed from one interlocutor to the next. Later participants could respond to what the others had offered earlier. In effect, it would become a traveling symposium until everything said was finally edited and put together in book form.

As an inveterate practitioner and teacher of literary translation, I was eager to engage those similarly committed, especially those writers not used to commenting widely on their practice. For convenience' sake, I chose the ones most geographically accessible whose work I admired and who had some notion of my own translating efforts. That way the fraternal nature of the enterprise permitted me to follow personal, even idiosyncratic paths beyond the lair of the craftsman's secrets I was prying into. And so perhaps new ground was occasionally broken, with unlooked-for results. If I was not uniformly successful in drawing forth richer material than what a translator was momentarily willing to share, the limitations of my open method—or lack of method—may be partly to blame. These are not unrelated to the notorious disadvantages of the spontaneous taped interview: the impossibility of much studied preparation; the lack of time in which to follow through on complex questions; and the sometimes apparent thinness of the artifice of conversational exchange as compared to the single-author text. Disadvantages such as these are inherent in any project seeking extemporarily for otherwise unobtainable insights from highly diverse temperaments.

Other difficulties arose from the partial or total unavailability of some of the translators. For one, there was W. S. Merwin, with whom I had had a rewarding public conversation at Brown University, the tape of which was subsequently lost. Other translators were unable to complete the necessary arrangements for preliminary talk to develop fruitfully. In such ways I lost the chance to include the polylingual Estonian poet Aleksis Rannit, the Israeli poet T. Carmi, and the four Americans, William J. Smith, Ruth Whitman, Constance Carrier, and Ruth Feldman. Nevertheless, all of them responded generously to queries about their craft, and so helped me to point my questions to the poet-translators who were available. I would have been pleased to engage such translators as Robert Bly, Richard Howard, Willis Barnstone, Allen Mandelbaum, and William Arrowsmith, but conditions proved unfavorable for conversation according to the format I had set up.

Obviously my aim could not have been to present a comprehensive or even a judiciously selective account of the subject. Rather, and more likely, it was to uncover certain of the unperceived dynamics of poetic translation at work among the practitioners themselves. And the practice, as might be expected, proved varied enough. Willard Trask had been a published translator for sixty years. Besides his versions of novels and philosophical works from the Spanish, German, and French, he had done into English over five hundred medieval Portuguese poems. The poet John Hollander is a trained critical theorist as well as a translator of Yiddish. Poet-novelist and scholar of Islamic literature, Herbert Mason is noted for a remarkable verse imitation from *Gilgamesh*, the Akkadian epic. Pablo Neruda's poetry and Federico García Lorca's *Poet in New*

York are as well known in English through Ben Belitt's translations as are the plays of Molière through Richard Wilbur's. Robert Fitzgerald's versions of Homer's and Vergil's epics are standard texts in American colleges. Though contemporary Russian fiction, including *Doctor Zhivago*, was the main province of Max Hayward, he also served as principal informant to British and American poets translating their Russian counterparts into English. The novelist-critic Edmund Keeley is a skilled and assiduous translator of the contemporary Greek poets. And Latin America's celebrated poet Octavio Paz is distinguished for his theories of translation as well as for his bilingual editions of Portuguese, French, and American poets. The British poets Michael Hamburger and Christopher Middleton are responsible, between them, for continuing and quite different engagements with Friedrich Hölderlin and the modern German poets and fiction writers. The gamut of approaches represented here can be taken as typical of the poet-translator alert to the always beckoning possibilities of new poetic transformations.

All eleven participants were engaged long enough in such transformative processes to articulate their views over a wide spectrum of achievement. Each translator examined the transcript of his conversation and made appropriate revisions—some radically, others quite minimally. Several acknowledged that much unvoiced thought and feeling during decades of solitary practice emerged in ways they would not otherwise have expressed. What shortcomings exist in these exchanges resulting from limited discernment I must claim to be of my own instigating. Whatever virtues and agreeable surprises are contained in them I hope will be manifest and attributed to the good nature and zealous commitment of the participants.

Introduction

This is a personal book on a subject whose theory is so wide ranging that it may be impossible to locate fully, and yet whose practice is so universally accepted that casual readers often mistake a translation for its original. No one is ever likely to have the last word about translation when even to ask productive questions requires a predisposition for penetrating its basic intricacies. Perhaps, then, to take translation personally— that is, to account for it as a matter of one's particular intentions and practice—may be the best way of demonstrating its ubiquity and elusiveness. In this spirit I begin with a brief survey of my experience with translation over several decades, one that may be matched with the reports of others in the conversations that follow.

Like others with an early multilingual awareness, I recall certain linguistic occasions that seem crucial to my becoming a poet and a translator. And like others again, I remember being forced to translate before I knew any foreign language or even had enough of my own English to write a letter home from camp.

On my mother's side, Yiddish, Polish, and German were spoken; on my father's, Hebrew, Spanish, Arabic, Yiddish, some Italian, a bit of French. As a child I kept listening to all the jabber. Nona, my paternal grandmother, was illiterate. Barely able to sign her name, she spoke three languages fluently: Arabic to her children, when she didn't want me to understand; Spanish or Ladino, when the immediate family came together; and Yiddish, for the in-laws exclusively. Her English was virtually nonexistent.

At seven, in Hebrew school, I picked up enough Hebrew to convert bits of the Bible into stammering Yiddish. Much later, in Israel, I got along on the same family Yiddish I hadn't spoken for thirty years. My language capability was always a residual learning: nonsystematic, preadolescent, half-hatched in the family nest.

The picture had a literary aspect too. At thirteen I gave up Conan Doyle for Hart Crane and T. S. Eliot, reading for the magic of their special language. The curiously evocative sounds and bizarre word pictures were what teachers called poems. In mouthing them I convinced myself I was mimicking still another foreign language. I saw that one might use words to invent something personal and magical. At the same time, I took to studying French and Spanish with a passion, and continued to translate Spanish poems and drama sporadically over the years.

In college I started Attic Greek, Latin, German, and Russian in my freshman year. Though I never mastered German I learned enough of it to remove natives from their homes during World War II and to provide billets for American soldiers. College German also gave me a start on Kafka and Rilke; of Russian I retained only what it took to sing "Styenka Razin" and to direct deported Russians out of Germany after the war.

My brush with languages seemed part of the business of becoming a poet, a continual self-renewing act. Head full of intimate-sounding alien words, I wrote poems with obscure resonances. The trick, like the ventriloquist's, was to project one's own voice and have it echoed back through a different though sympathetic other voice—the voice that could be re-created by imitating or translating another poet. That way I could assume one alter ego after another, something like voice-masks or personae, as Pound called them.

I can offer two instances of how this game worked for me some years later. The first concerns the Spanish Renaissance dramatist Pedro Calderón de la Barca (1600–1681); the other, Fernando Pessoa (1888–1935), Portugal's best poet since Camoens.

While living in Mallorca in 1958 I had a letter from Eric Bentley. He was collecting German, French, Spanish, and Italian classical drama in new translations, and was asking American poets—W. S. Merwin, Richard Wilbur, Robert Lowell, among others—to create something a bit better than readable versions of the old plays. Would I try Calderón? By chance, I had already begun to translate Calderón's basic honor play, *A secreto agravio, secreta venganza* (*Secret Vengeance for Secret Insult*), working three to five hours a day in a garden of ever-blooming roses and yellow-fringed mimosas. I had been led to Spain in the hope of recouping my college Spanish by doing translation as a literary exercise. If I worked well I might eventually be able to answer the shibboleth of the romance language departments that putting classical poetic drama into modern English is untrustworthy, if not pointless, because it is bound to misrepresent the old language. The effort seemed worth making—to keep alive the classics at a time when foreign literature was coming to be read more and more by specialists only. If Shakespeare in performance was far better known in Russia than in England or the United States, Boris Pasternak's translations were the reason why this might be so.

Implicit in the challenge was the possibility that a good translation could bring what was irreplaceable in the original together with what was missing from it. If I were successful, the translation would provide a new context in English that had not existed before. Such a transformation might be generated from the raw materials of the original through the word order natural to contemporary English. There seemed no use in doing a translation unless I were going to create a new work. There might be other translations, but there could not be another like my own. In the end, it would be a work in which the translator's imagination reflected that of the original author's. Wallace Stevens had said it: "The moon follows the sun like a French translation of a Russian novel."

Grand aims, superlative intentions—and all chastened by a few mornings' labor on the opening lines of *A secreto agravio*. No need to rehearse the details here; they are treated at length elsewhere.[1] Essentially I was learning how wide was the breach between freedom and necessity. Having to give up trying to imitate the varied verse patterns of the Spanish, I would have to invent a new measure to approximate them all. The sinewy, quick-moving, bare quality of language was what had fascinated me in the Spanish; and this was what I found missing in the general run of English translations. To create such a tonality without sacrificing verse to prose, I invented a flexible syllabic line, patterned on the octosyllabic *romance*, but different from the model (in which a syllable is sometimes omitted, sometimes added) in that it permitted a regular accentual beat to emerge: a variety of trimeter, tetrameter, and pentameter lines that does not offend the English ear but is strange enough to suggest the Spanish norm. This was the measure I adopted for the next four Calderón plays I translated.

After *Secret Vengeance* I undertook a miracle play, *La devoción de la cruz* (*Devotion to the Cross*). Camus had put it into French prose but as far as I knew no English translation existed. After the war its *credo ad absurdum* theme would appeal to the sensitive reader who might even come to regard it as Calderón's most "contemporary" play. But there were certain inherent problems in trying to maintain plausibility. The quick juxtapositions of comic exchanges with long soliloquies imposed on one another by dueling antagonists make tonal credibility impossible. The extreme absurdity framing the plight of the religious bandit-hero upsets the balance between comic and serious elements. This awkwardness is especially notable at the end of the play when the incestuous brother and sister are unexpectedly hauled off to heaven on their totemic cross. But the pathos of the victim-hero's triumph after death, his curious attachment to his sister, and his raw confrontations with a tyrannical father, allow for sharper conflicts to emerge than in those plays where tone and theme are more deliberately weighted against each other.

If one were seeking unified tone and a self-fulfilling theme, one would go to *El alcalde de Zalamea* (*The Mayor of Zalamea*) and *La dama duende* (*The Phantom Lady*), the plays I translated subsequently. The intrigue and semicomic tone in both lead to highly charged dénouements, giving a more immediate sense of unity than in the other two plays. There is subtler characterization as well as greater plot interest; yet the time-bound theme seems to tie up the characters in situations that are more routine than in the cruder *Secret* and the more bizarre *Devotion*.

To overcome a prolonged siege of asthma in Portugal in 1968, I started on *La vida es sueño* (*Life Is a Dream*), a play I had admired for many years. At some point I must have read through all thirteen English translations, from Archbishop Trench's to the Raine-Nadal version, which was being published in London just as I was completing my own. Hill and Wang, who had published my *Calderón: Four Plays* (1961), issued *Life Is a Dream* in 1970. The play was adapted by BBC-Radio Four in London for production in September of that year, and again in February 1971. It is Calderón's best-known work and perhaps his most viable as a dramatic production.

The language is formal and stylized, though not as complex as the language of *Hamlet*. Complexities of syntax, diction, and imagery fall into predictable sequences. Like a many-petaled rose, each petal opens just enough to let out its curious fragrance. But the rose never opens fully. In spite of its limitations the play contains high eloquence and pirouetting magniloquence. Virtuosity of this sort, occurring in the soliloquies, makes these elements jut out like statues bare and proud among trimmed hedges in a formal park.

Although much in the play seems fixed by conventions familiar to readers of the Spanish *comedia*, the technical rarity lies in Calderón's inventiveness, his baroque imagination. *Hipogrifo violento*—"wild hippogriff"—the opening words of the play, and possibly the most famous in Spanish literature, are impossible to translate literally. *Hippogriff* sounds too much like *hypocrite*. My alternative was a calculated dodge: "Mad horse, half griffin." Other problems arise out of Calderón's hyperboles and his inveterate word-and-idea punning. And yet mannerisms of this sort are perhaps not uncongenial to a generation raised on Eliot and Donne. When it was not dramatically feasible to stick close to the Spanish, I invented a phrase out of what appeared to be the same rhetorical tradition. Occasionally I found myself sharpening a meaning. There is the famous couplet concluding Segismundo's soliloquy at the end of Act Two: "Que toda la vida es sueño, / y los sueños, sueños son," from which I derived the sensible but perhaps inelegant gloss, "for all of life's a dream, and dreams / themselves are only part of dreaming."

My other example of a prolonged fix upon a translation subject is Fernando Pessoa. Traveling through the Algarve in 1963 I heard of the poet for the first time. In the seaside town of Praia da Rocha, in the Penguin Inn (a bar run by a South African couple) I heard a fisherman reciting some poetry. By chance I found myself sitting beside António Quadros, the literary man who'd written a book about Pessoa. Quadros picked up where the fisherman left off with more verses of what turned out to be Pessoa's. Later in Lisbon I was urged by other Portuguese writers to translate Pessoa's poetry, then virtually unknown in English. At first their Pessoa put me off: a vaguely anachronistic, Pirandellian figure, inhabiting a set of four distinct but totally made-up poets he called heteronyms in order to make the orthonym—Fernando Pessoa himself—credible. But the more I read the heteronymic works the more attractive seemed his tough elusive vision, the ray of hope barely visible in the bleakness of his lines. In his last years Pessoa's work was just being discovered, piecemeal, by the younger generation in Portugal. As one poet later told me, it was a work that made the Lisbon chambermaids speak a different Portuguese from their mothers.

Pessoa's appeal starts with his novel use of Whitman, especially in the poetry of his loudest heteronym, Álvaro de Campos, a fictitious ship's engineer from Glasgow writing in Portuguese. "Maritime Ode," a thirty-page poem, could not have existed without Whitman. Not only does Campos-Pessoa use Whitman's free forms (daring enough for a Portuguese poet in 1918), but also, as a rather different personality who assumes the American poet's voice, he turns out a complexly ironic portrait of a modern schizophrenic. It is probably Pessoa's most powerful poem, portraying that disturbed white-collar worker we all know (the legendary madman famous since Gogol), whose meek smile hides explosive fantasies, whose apparent peaceableness barely keeps the lid on his suicidal and homicidal tendencies. "Maritime Ode" clears the way for the uninhibited "I" in Portuguese poetry. The phenomenon of the poem rivals, in effect, the appearance in mid-nineteenth-century America of "Song of Myself." Campos and Whitman seethe with raucous denunciations often subsiding into a murky sentimentality, but the energy and clarity of poetic vision in each instance is overpowering. Whitman was aware of the split between the I and the self, and Campos in his ode to Whitman displays his love and envy of the American poet, seeing him as a brother and comrade who might have served as still another Pessoa heteronym.

I had had a Whitman period too, but translating Pessoa helped me to think of the American poet in a different light; working tentatively in a free style, I was brought to a boil by the Whitmanesque Pessoa. Through the translations I saw the possibilities of using a variety of voices to carry to completion a long work of my own. *Four Springs*, a book-length poem, appeared in 1972, the year following the publication of my early Pessoa translations.

The working principle I followed was to tilt the poetry toward American vernacular rather than faceless common English usage. Perhaps this made my translation suspect in Britain, but I was not trying to limit Pessoa to American readers. It seemed clear that Whitman was crucial in shaping Pessoa's liberated poetic voice, especially that of Álvaro de Campos and Alberto Caeiro. Had he been writing in English today, he might easily have adopted the American idiom for his odes. The vernacular, with its contractions, separable verbs, repetitions of informal monosyllabic counters like *get*, *do*, *have*, *make*, and crude localisms— these were the right means to impersonate the heteronyms that had freed Portuguese poetry.

My translations of Calderón and Pessoa—and before them, of Federico García Lorca in the 1940s—made me aware that there was a need for more direct and realistic information on what translators actually do. Whatever translators think, their work cannot proceed simply from a single theory about how to do it. The complex and irrational serving of exigency while calibrating word-by-word minutiae makes them uncomfortable with all theories. Nor do mottoes help muffle the small crushing voice they hear whispering, "What you're doing is ridiculous because it's absolutely impossible." To which they will invariably agree, but with a touch of Kafkan paradoxicality, as Willard Trask suggests when asserting, "Impossible, of course—that's why I do it." Edward FitzGerald's light-hearted preference for "the live dog" over "the dead lion" expresses the common, mitigating faith of translators in the enduring vitality of language.

What is one's relation to a job—a job one wants to do well? One must first believe it can be done. But how the belief is sustained through all the self-abnegations of translation and mistranslation is a psychological mystery only translators themselves can reveal—and then only partially. But reveal it they will, if only after the work has been published, when they no longer feel haunted by the dark antagonist of the elusive and beloved text, a form of the other voice. For, evidently, love of the created work, its theme and language, is a sustaining force too. A translator's experience of personal loss, supported by the affirming presence of a friend, as Herbert Mason discovered in preparing his *Gilgamesh* version, can also keep one going. Crucial as such factors are to perseverance, they bring about a still more vital effect: that of influencing the special shape the work takes, measured by the degree of freedom needed to restore the text. John Hollander shows how a working translator, in minding, mending, emending, and transcending a text, may learn to become a poet himself. The same activity enforces the conflation of spirit that makes Jonson or Campion a new Catullus and permits Dante Gabriel Rossetti to assume his predecessor's voice in doing the "Stony Sestina," that exceedingly close rendering of the earlier Dante's lines.

What part of their own voice, then, do poets discover in another's, or what of the other's do they put into their own? And what is a poet's voice? Is it some arbitrary locus made out of pressured words, the projection of some imaginative possibility vocalized, as the self is, to stand for the individual? Is translation as self-transcendence still another version of the paradox: to know yourself, lose yourself in the other? If voice is the instrument making it possible for poets to continue writing by giving immediacy and validity to whatever gift they possess, it also exists in the constant collaboration between the language of the living and the language of the dead. Poets come to know that voice is both one's own and not one's own. As Antonio Machado observes, the poet, perceiving all the unbidden echoes in his personal language, realizes that his voice is not "mine" but "ours." He senses that it resounds, as a collaborative instrument, and that the collaborators are the literary masters of many human languages, including many he does not know, as well as the special languages of trees, waters, and illiterate grandmothers.

Such psycholinguistic and psycholiterary processes are of first importance in understanding what gets put into what, and how one literary work actually nurtures another into being. Equally significant, at a time of extraordinary and prolific translation activity, is that really knowing these processes may help to end the sterile old battle between advocates of faithfulness or libertarianism. Nor is it true, as opponents to all such polemics like to say, that what counts finally is not *how* the work comes into existence but *that* it exists. To learn from translators what goes into their efforts opens a new terrain, conceivably lying somewhere between letter and spirit, when it is truly mapped, in the game we call literary creation.

1 / Willard Trask

EH   I would like to ask first how you began as a translator.

WT   I've always been interested in poetry, and I suppose I'm a disappointed poet. I've tried, but never done anything in poetry that really lived up to my standards. Anyway, I became especially interested in medieval poetry. And I realized that medieval poetry was an international phenomenon. (In order to . . . not to understand it, but at least to get the most out of it in one language, you should know what's being done in other languages. There's a good deal of communication, too, between the languages, which would justify that.) I had the luck, when my father died, to inherit some money. So I took it and went to France and lived there as long as I could—about seven years—and studied languages. I'd been born in Germany; my parents were Americans, my father was an engineer. He was working in Russia and Mother was sent to Germany as the nearest civilized place to have a baby, so I had a sort of childish German. Mother taught me French; that was the only language I really knew well. I went to high school in Panama and learned some Spanish there. Those were my starts at the time when I went to France to stay.

EH   You spoke English at home, though?

WT   Oh, I spoke English, yes. Father and Mother were both American. So, there in Paris I ran into a Russian who had the Russian gift for languages raised to the point of genius. His name was George Marguliès. And I collaborated with him on some translations from Chinese. He knew the Chinese and gave me—verbally—literal translations. I put them into English, and we published them in *Asia Magazine*. We also

11

found that we were interested in the same things. We were both reading the French Renaissance poets, and he said, "Well, you must learn Spanish because you'll love Lope de Vega." So I learned Spanish out of love of Lope de Vega. That accounts for the languages. I picked them up essentially because of my interest in medieval forms. For example, I learned medieval Portuguese. I wouldn't starve in Portugal, but I can't conduct a literary conversation in modern Portuguese. When I came back from abroad, my money having run out—it was the Depression—I was trying to get a job, but I thought that with all of those languages (by that time I'd added Italian and was working on Portuguese) and the fact that I did know English, I ought to be able to do translation a bit. So, this is rather amusing, having to do with publication. . . . I knew Bill Soskin, who was a book reviewer for the *Evening Post*. He gave me quite a few letters of introduction to publishers. So I went around, and the phrase, "Don't call us, we'll call you," hadn't been invented then, but it's the equivalent of what was said to me. I never did hear from them. It was five years from the time I started out that I got my first translation. Meanwhile, I had been supporting myself as a proofreader for printing plants.

EH Proofreader for newspapers?

WT No, a regular commercial printing house for books. It was Wolf and Company, a huge printing plant in downtown New York, printing all kinds of books. But eventually, through one of Bill Soskin's letters, I was introduced to a young editor at Doubleday. He was an Irishman, a very good editor who published and printed novels of several people in their twenties who later became well known. He died young, unfortunately. I went and told him my tale of woe, and he said: "Your situation reminds me of my ex-wife; she too knew six languages."

EH Sounds like a curse.

WT "It gave people an inferiority complex," he went on, "and she found it hard to get work." Then he said, "I'm going to give you work." Lo and behold, a few weeks later he sent me a novel by Ramón Sender, *Crónica del alba*, which I still think is one of the most charming books I've ever translated.

Since then I've never been without a translation; but, if it hadn't been for running into that particular editor, and his having had that kind of an ex-wife, I think I might still be beating the pavements.

EH I doubt that, but it was a good break. . . . Then the Sender book was the first book you translated in its entirety as a commission?

WT As a job for a publisher. When I was in college I remember translating some poems of Baudelaire. I ran across one of them among some old papers the other day and it was pretty bad. I don't think I started very well. I don't know, though. I suppose it was something I wanted to do.

EH May I ask: What are the motives for a person to set up as a translator? You've partly answered that, I think. Would you like to say any more?

WT I could write and was, essentially, a literary man. But, what I've found out about it is that though I could undoubtedly at some point—several points—have gotten a job as an editor in a publishing house, being a translator gives you what I call an "illusion of freedom." All you need is a text to translate, a typewriter, a chair to sit in, a table to type on. Actually, you can take the typewriter and go to New Hampshire; you can go anywhere. . . . So it's this illusion of freedom that makes it worthwhile. To me. Although as a living, it's been poverty wages.

EH That kind of freedom, of course, people have who write, or who think they're writing, other things. But it would seem to be, as you said before, part of the literary person's job.

WT Yes.

EH Though some people don't have or can't use languages, therefore can't be translators. The impulse, would you say, is the same as that of someone who wants to write a novel?

WT No, I wouldn't say so, because I once tried to write a novel. When you're writing a novel—I never got one written, at least one that was any good, but I know what you're trying to do—you're obviously writing about people or places, something or other, but what you are essentially doing is expressing yourself. Whereas when you translate you're not expressing yourself. You're performing a technical stunt.

EH A "technical stunt"—that's a good term. Can you say something more about it?

WT Actually, I think, though I came to it rather late, I might have been an actor. And when I became one, I realized that the translator and the actor had to have the same kind of talent. What they both do is to take something of somebody else's and put it over as if it were their own. I think you have to have that capacity. So in addition to the technical stunt, there is a psychological workout, which translation involves: something like being on stage. It does something entirely different from what I think of as creative poetry writing.

EH   So it's a little like taking on a persona, as an actor does.

WT   Exactly.

EH   That's interesting to me because of what it suggests about an intermediate area between the work itself and the delivery of it or the translation of it. That intermediate area is the psychological preparation to do it, which is all that goes into . . .

WT   I'd rather say, "the psychological experience of doing it." I'm a great believer in "a job's a job, and do it," and in what happens while you do it. I don't read a whole book through before I translate it. I read enough of it to know that I'm interested enough in it to do what I'm going to do. Then I start in and it happens to me as I'm going on with it.

EH   In a sense like any reader, as you do it you are led on. . . .

WT   Yes, it's the carrot in front of the donkey. But I'd love to translate *Madame Bovary*. It's the greatest novel ever written, and probably the most impossible prose to translate. I'd love to have a try at it. So if I were to do that, I'd almost know it by heart before I started.

EH   So with a book like *Madame Bovary* there'd be a difference because you'd already know it.

WT   It's that carrot again. I'd know what was going to happen, but I'd still have the carrot—my intense admiration for it.

EH   Yes, I see. Well, there's a difference between the novels that you've translated and the other books. You've translated many novels?

WT   I've translated quite a number. I've translated one very minor work of Thomas Mann, *The Black Swan*. It's one of his later things but really not worth very much. His regular translator, Mrs. Lowe-Porter, was ill and couldn't do it. Knopf asked me to do it, and I did. I'm no great admirer of Mann, but I thought, "You know, someone's got to translate Mann, so maybe you really ought to do it." One of those things.

EH   What were some other novels?

WT   One about the Middle Ages, by Zoë Oldenbourg. I enjoyed doing that.

EH What was the title?

WT *The World Is Not Enough.* That was for Pantheon Books. Pantheon Books was then Helen and Kurt Wolff. Through that connection I was later given Auerbach to translate, then Curtius, which I also enjoyed doing very much, but obviously for very different reasons and in a very different way. I found one very rewarding thing: I met Auerbach, who was teaching at Yale. A charming man and, at the same time, devoted—perhaps you've some idea of the late nineteenth-century Continental style. Charming and gentlemanly. And I can say much of the same of Eliade, whose books I've translated too. He writes most of his scientific books in French, although he's a Romanian—but he sticks to Romanian for his novels and short stories. One of the difficulties then is—you know, as an actor you don't really have to kill the king. So I don't really have to *understand* "personae," or things like that, in order to translate them. I mean—I know that *persona* is a term in classical rhetoric. I know the definition of it in that usage; but what has been made of it—or is being made of it—since, is simply not material to my purposes. But then when you go out into the world with the reputation that you know these things people find you out and are disappointed.

EH Well, there are two things there: one is that you went on translating from essays or criticism to novels—or were you doing them about the same time?

WT No, it's the other way around: all the first translations were novels.

EH . . . And you met the authors, like Auerbach, which is a little different from the experience of most translators usually. I take it you didn't meet Mann or Oldenbourg.

WT No, I didn't. Well, actually, if I had met Mann and if I'd dared to, I would have suggested to him that it wasn't true of American workmen that they had fine hands because they wore white gloves. That's what he says in *The Black Swan!* Actually, when reading Auerbach in German—as you probably know, German can be written with an extraordinary degree of sounding like something and meaning nothing. When I first met Auerbach, I went up to Yale from Manhattan. We had a conference about the passages I couldn't make any sense of, and some of them he couldn't make sense of either. He said, "Quite frankly, I don't remember what I was trying to say." So then he'd say something else instead, for me to translate.

EH Did he rewrite or did he explain?

WT No, *viva voce*. . . . With Curtius there were a few problems of that sort, but he was in Germany and I wrote to him there, so that was about it.

EH Did either of these men see your work in English? Did they have a chance to see what you published of theirs?

WT I don't know if Curtius did. Auerbach did. Several chapters of the *Mimesis* came out in *Partisan Review* before it was published as a book. Incidentally, I can throw a bit of a sidelight on editors in connection with this. One of the editors of *Partisan Review* had a conference with Auerbach at which I was present, before they were going to publish his chapter on Homer, where he refers to Ulysses as a "legendary" figure. The editor's question was why did he say *legendary*. "Why don't you say *mythical*—that's what everyone's talking about nowadays—*mythical*." And Auerbach answered, "I said *legendary* because I meant *legendary*."

EH *Mimesis* is a book I know well because I've used it as a basic text at Brown in teaching criticism, and I've had students' reactions to it. The typical reaction is, "This is enjoyable reading," mainly from students who otherwise think criticism has to be obscure. It's that aspect, the limberness of the style, which people notice and take as an invitation to the book's readability.

WT That's interesting, because after all it is, or should be, the dullest form of criticism, aside from the difficulties—*explication de texte*, which is word-for-word—and yet he makes it not dull at all.

EH In that way he's a pioneer—in showing what can be done in lightening that form of criticism, which has now returned to favor, especially among the French critics, although the dullness hasn't departed. . . . It seems that Portuguese medieval poetry has been a lifelong interest of yours, from the beginning.

WT No, I wouldn't say lifelong—but from the time when I discovered it, when I was about thirty. Portuguese was the last European language I learned. Some initiate set me on to it.

EH I see, and you've stuck with it all this time.

WT Yes.

EH Well, I was going to ask: there are obviously certain foreign authors who are sympathetic to one in translating. Is this also true of languages?

WT It's true of languages. The language I like least is German and the one I like best is French. Whether that's because to a certain extent I have the remains of an eighteenth-century logical-minded fellow in me, or that kind of mind to which German is antithetical, I don't know. It's probably for some such reason of temperament as that.

EH I want now to go on to ask you what the differences may have been in your experience between translating novels and other prose, between translating prose and poetry, and living languages as against dead languages, or earlier forms of living languages. That's a big list to confront you with, I admit.

WT Well, to take the last one first. If it's a *dead* language, you might as well not try to translate it.

EH By *dead* I mean, of course, a nonspoken language, like Latin or Attic Greek.

WT I should say the difference is something of this sort: if you don't go to Paris every year, no dictionary is going to tell you what words have sprung up there. Whereas once you know Latin or medieval Portuguese you obviously *know* the language. In the modern language there'd be more vocabulary difficulties than grammatical difficulties, so I suppose you're safer in a "dead" language.

EH Well, when you translate from the already formulated, nonchanging old language, do you have a feeling about the kind of English it ought to go into?

WT I certainly don't feel it ought to go into any pseudoantique English. But I'm very strong in the belief that one of the important things is the order in which thoughts enter minds. As nearly as possible—although you certainly can't do it for very long with German, or at all with Latin, as far as that goes—one should try to keep somewhere near the word order of the original in the translation. I mean this can be done by substituting other constructions, but I think it's very important that what is thought first in, say, the Latin text should be thought first in the English sentence.

EH Even though the practice may go against the English word order?

WT Well, you can't do it every time, by any manner of means. But you could do it by using some clause or phrase, or something of that sort. Do you know Ortega y Gasset's essay on translation?

EH Yes, but I haven't read it recently.

WT   Well, he says there are two kinds of translation. One is the kind that's usually approved of, and that is one that sounds as if it were originally written in the language into which it is being translated. The other kind, which he's plugging, is one that gives you the *experience* of the language from which the translation is made.

EH   Does that mean that it must *sound* like a translation?

WT   It sounds like a translation. It sounds like Latin with English words. But obviously you can only do this to a certain extent or no one would read it. But I'm very strong on trying it. And I think that the way you can do it is to have your English be *so* English in the passages that don't matter that you can get away, where it does matter, with something foreign. And, of course, gradually in the course of generations—I mean everything is going to have to be translated again in another fifty years from now—gradually I think that people will feel at home with more foreign constructions than they now admit. Do you know that in Selden's *Table Talk*, he rises in wrath against the King James version of the Bible? He says that no such Hebrew idioms were ever thrust upon the unhappy English language; while a hundred years later the King James version became the greatest work of English prose! Thirty years after it appeared it's considered full of Hebraisms, and as a matter of fact I was in some place where there was a Gideon Bible and I looked at the preface to it, and the American revisers of 1880 something-or-other were still complaining that the King James version has Hebraisms in it!

EH   This obviously depends on the strategy of the translator, as you say, and his way of "placing" things, but saying there are only two kinds of translation is obviously not true. There may often be only two points of view, but when it comes to practice it's hard to think that you can sustain a totally "faithful" as against a totally "liberal" view.

WT   Well, I don't suppose we'll ever get this sort of thing settled. But when it comes to my own choice as a reader of translations, take an instance: I don't know any Sanskrit, but when I want to read some Indian scripture or other, I try to get one of those old translations that are practically trots, make no pretense at being literary, but are simply interlinear translations. You know, those trots we used to have for Latin which had the Latin words printed underneath and rearranged the English. I'd prefer to fight with something like that instead of having someone else's "beauty" to cope with!

EH Well, that's a professional attitude. I've been reading a book by a man named Adams called *Proteus: His Lies, His Truth.*[2]

WT Sounds like a good title.

EH He's a man with wide cultural and literary interests who writes well. Many of the questions he raises have a strong literary challenge. One of the things that struck me was his saying that a translation can succeed on many different levels because the translation has many levels of equivalence. That is, it needn't succeed on all levels, because equivalence, he feels, is a matter of having made thousands of linguistic decisions between the two languages involved. So that the end-product might finally be very interesting and yet not really be faithful, even though very *close* to the original.

WT There are linguistic decisions to make, but except in the rarest of instances each one of them is a compromise. The thing about translations is that you're licked before you start, so then you do the best you can.

EH So you begin with the idea that it's impossible and therefore you go on and do it. That's a kind of mad-Roger strategy.

WT Yes, I'd think so. Actually I never read a translation—say from French or from Spanish—except that nowadays it's hard to get hold of some of the Latin American books sometimes. But I wouldn't think of reading a translation from any language that I know, if I can get hold of the original.

EH Well, that accounts for a number of things. For instance, the prejudice against translation on the part of teachers of modern languages. They don't see why people shouldn't bother to learn the original. So they're impatient, at least in this country, with English translations. Of course, there is something to what the modern language teachers and others feel about translation which is partly justified, if you think of the adaptors instead of the translators. People are put off by someone like Edward FitzGerald, say, whose observation about "the live dog [being] better than the dead lion" implies something which the literalists cannot abide. It implies that "faithful" translation is hopeless and something much less "true" to the original text is inevitable. But Calderón in FitzGerald's version is deliberately invented as a Restoration dramatist in English, not as a seventeenth-century Golden Age creator of formal *comedias*.

WT I think that's partly true of adapting a play; but suppose the first person trying to convey into English some Japanese haiku should say, "Well, there's no such form in English. We're going to do it in couplets."

EH That's happened, of course. Exactly that.

WT But less "sensitive" people would decide to do it in English in three lines and even in twenty-one syllables, and that's worked. That's the Haiku Society of America and thousands of people are writing haikus. I can't imagine they're all good, though some seem quite good indeed. That's what I mean when I talk about what Ortega says and what I try to do. I think you've got to try and get in all the foreignness you can—all that you can get in and get away with.

EH And as you say, it's not to sound like something you might have written yourself.

WT No, but I don't know. The *Rubáiyát* I think is a very fine poem and I guess it's as much FitzGerald as it's Omar Khayyám. I can't judge between the translation and the original, but it turns out to be a beautiful piece of work. I mean, I suppose he was ready to do it because there was a classical precedent to utter skepticism. So if there hadn't been a classical precedent for it, he'd probably have thought it was too Persian and wouldn't have done it, or have done it in a different way.

EH That's interesting because he seemed to be trying to do just that with Calderón—follow the path of free-handed adaptation while sticking to the important lines of the play. But Calderón is closer to us than Khayyám; he's just past Shakespeare's time, though sometimes a bit more like our Restoration dramatists. The kind of thing FitzGerald tries with Khayyám he doesn't get away with in Calderón. The general play reader, if he were shown FitzGerald's *Life Is a Dream*, would think it entertaining, and even sounding a bit like a foreign classic, but it's so far away from the Spanish tragic genre of *La vida es sueño* that it seems unacceptable as a Spanish play in English. Maybe there's room for it, if you think that adaptations can be as useful as translations, as they are obviously in the theater. But that's another question.

Now I'd like to ask you more about your translations from the medieval Portuguese. About the Portuguese: you've done about a thousand out of three or four thousand poems—a matter of winnowing them out. What are the poems like?

WT Well, they're like Scottish folk songs, or Burns, perhaps—that's the nearest thing I can think of to compare them with in our literature—

and a lot of them, including the best ones, are girls' songs, that is, the speakers are girls—although they were all composed by men. It's a regular folk form, as in Burns too, say. And there are two kinds formally: some are in a dance form, with repetitions, and the others in a four-to-five-line stanza with a one- or two-line refrain, where the psychology becomes more interesting. Those were the first I did—the psychologically charming ones. I don't know if I mentioned that those are by King Denis, an almost exact contemporary of Dante's, and they're too charming for words—the few that I did first.

EH   Do you think King Denis was one of the best?

WT   Oh, easily. Some of the others are better than Denis at the more nearly folk form, the dance thing. But it's very hard to say, because since he was a king, all his poems, thirty-odd, are preserved. Other people have only one or two, five or six.

EH   Were these written for music?

WT   Oh yes. We have one manuscript that consists of seven songs by one man and six of them have musical notations, four decipherable now; out of the whole two or three thousand, those are the only tunes we have. The poet, of course, was also the composer, as among the Provençal troubadours.

EH   When you translate them, are you aware of any music?

WT   I'm aware of rhythm, very much so. . . .

EH   There's the dinner bell, Willard. I'm sorry that it breaks into our rhythm here. Can we pick the conversation up later?

WT   Be my guest, Edwin. Of course.

2 / John Hollander

EH You have done translations and written poems, and have perhaps even been translated. So, to begin, I'd like to have your views on how a translation is made, and if it's possible, to relate this to a theory of translation as I know you've written about it. The distinction is between thinking of translating as a prescriptive exercise and translating as something in the making, a live performance.

It might be best to talk first about your essay in Brower's book,[3] where it appears that you're trying to establish a way of looking at translation that would facilitate thinking of it realistically as a "version" rather than a faithful rendering.

JH Yes. I wrote that a long time ago and, I think, a little brashly. Certainly at too great a length. I was interested in trying to show that any particular literary translation will be a version based on the literary style of the translator. Even if he thinks he is surrendering everything to the meaning that he wants to embody, he will all the more be betraying stylistic conventions, so that the only thing to do is consciously decide upon a stylistic analogue for that of the original and carry the meaning over to that.

EH Interesting, but I don't remember your saying that in your essay.

JH No. In the essay I brought up the difference between Latin prose composition, where there was a correct answer—where you were trying to approximate to Cicero in Latin and did your exercises—and the translating of a Ciceronian sentence into English, which had a great many possible solutions.

EH Yes, I thought that very valuable as a start.

JH In a larger sense, all literary translations are "versions" that way. And what I just said to you was perhaps an afterthought on that essay fifteen years or so later.

EH What's happened to your notion of a "version"?

JH I think it has implications for nontranslative writing as well. I think that a certain amount of self-awareness about style is absolutely necessary in learning how to write by learning *how* one is writing. What puts a lot of young poets off their true course is some sense that they're starting from scratch. And the relation of translation to original creative writing in any tradition is rather interesting. These questions have been raised in recent books on the subject. Robert Martin Adams raises that notion.[4] Frederic Will does too.[5]

EH In your essay when you bring in T. S. Eliot and the interpretive style and suggest that translation is interpretation, you evidently situate the whole drift of modernist poetry from Eliot and Pound as partly an active engagement with translation.

JH Well, I won't say that it was all ideological from modernism, although I know I did pick up that idea. No. Before having any real contact with modernism I simply felt obliged to do translations. That is, before I ever did poems of my own. The first undergraduate poems I published were translations of Baudelaire. I felt that translating Baudelaire was a necessary step in an apprenticeship. I don't know why and I don't know who told me.

EH I've often given my writing students exercises in translation or urged them to write versions of poems from other languages.

JH I had written humorous light verse in high school but never did anything I called a poem until after I'd translated Baudelaire.

EH I think I see a connection between what you just said about producing poetry via learning to translate and what you said before about deliberately choosing an analogue in order to make a translation, back of which is also your notion of translation as making versions of the original.

JH I think so, yes.

EH But then you said that you are no longer interested in doing translation.

JH I find myself no longer wanting to translate now.

EH Why is that?

JH   I don't know. My last experiences with it were most fortunate. The last things I did were a lot of poems from the Yiddish for an anthology by Irving Howe and Eliezer Greenberg.[6] In the course of that work I discovered the poet Moishe-Leib Halpern, and my translations of him were lucky. More than that, they seemed to help me develop a certain tonal mode in my own poems. That is, what I had to do to translate certain poems of Halpern's, I've now retained as a vocal element. Doing Halpern provided a way of unlocking certain things. My Yiddish isn't very good. It's learned, a secondary and artificial thing, since nobody spoke Yiddish in my family. But I knew some German and I'd been taught a little Hebrew, and I learned how Germanic Yiddish is transcribed in Hebrew letters. Also, I worked very closely with Irving Howe, who is a friend, and when there were difficulties he would discuss a word or two with me.

EH   I know that anthology; I contributed translations to it myself. How well does Howe know Yiddish?

JH   Very well. Perfectly, yes.

EH   But it's not "learned" Yiddish.

JH   No, it's native. He could point out the resonance of a particular Yiddish word, especially one with a Slavic origin or with a special use. I knew enough language to tell immediately whether it was a Yiddish word or a Hebrew word that had entered into Yiddish. This helped in separating out tone. I'd have to use a high diction, for example, to translate a resonant Hebrew abstraction, then shift to a very vibrant low diction sometimes, for other effects. I knew enough to see that immediately, although I cannot jabber the language. But I felt I didn't trust myself to translate that.

EH   Isn't it true that Yiddish is more of an oral, colloquial language than a literary language? My question is prompted by the fact that I picked up what Yiddish I know in my grandmother's house as a child. I didn't learn it as a literary language though I studied Hebrew in the Talmud Torah.

JH   Well, Yiddish has a short literary tradition, nineteenth-century mostly, and of course this foreshortens the poetic tradition in many strange ways.

EH   So that in translating Yiddish, for example, one is aware of the vernacular more than if one were translating German. Well, let me go back to something else, and perhaps ahead at the same time. The business of your learning something about the writing of poetry from first translating, then the business latterly of your having given up translation after suddenly making a momentous discovery with Halpern indicate that you have assimilated a great deal. It makes me think again that in the work of other poets—Pound and Eliot, say—translation is a large assimilated element.

JH   Oh, it's essential there, but Pound and Eliot are both poets with grave problems of originality and grave problems about confronting their lack of originality. It seems inevitable that they would propound. Like Longfellow they propound a corpus of poetry largely based on translation. *Corpus* in both cases. They are both, I think, much more like Longfellow than we've admitted.

EH   But doing what they did with translation, they paved the way for others to write differently.

JH   Well, yes, in one way. As far as I know, our greatest poet in the twentieth century, at least our greatest American poet, never did any translation: Wallace Stevens.

EH   But I always felt Stevens had assimilated French.

JH   He may intone a lot of French in his poems, but he doesn't sit down and do translations. I've stopped translating because it takes so much time. Also, I think there is so much indifferent verse translation going on now by people who don't have any particular skills in writing English verse but who proceed to translate from languages that they don't know. I am a little ashamed of some translating I have done from languages I don't know well enough. I have never translated from a language I didn't know at all: I won't do that. In the case of some translations of Voznesensky, I have worked from minimal Russian. I worked with Olga Carlisle on those. I did translate from the Russian text except that my Russian text was annotated after hours of going over it with her.

EH   But you hadn't studied Russian before?

JH   Yes, I'd studied some Russian.

EH   So you knew the grammar.

JH   I knew the grammar. As I say, I worked from the Russian text, which I could read, and I knew the grammar, but I don't know very much Russian. I know even less now. But I still am a little ashamed of having done that. Except that the versions turned out rather well.

EH   I was talking with Aleksis Rannit yesterday, and he illustrated rather pointedly the unexpected and unequal results of knowing and not knowing a language well. Yakobovich, a Russian poet jailed in Siberia for twenty-five years, spent his time there writing version after version of *Les Fleurs du Mal*. Aleksis reports that the final results were an abysmal failure. But another Russian poet, Fyodov Sologub, who knew much less French than Yakobovich, did a much quicker and vastly better job of translating Baudelaire. So. . . .

JH   There is another dimension to this matter. A very, very good poet can do a version of something from another language, even if he doesn't know the language. That is, he can write a poem based on somebody else's prose paraphrases of the thing. But this is purely and simply a matter of the translator's having a certain kind of poetic skill, a very rare thing to find. By and large, I disapprove of my having done translations from a language I didn't know well enough, and want now not to do that any more. I also feel I have done my bit to a degree, that is, helped out in certain projects. That Borges book [*pointing to it*] you have there is a unique case. I don't really know Spanish well. I can read it with a dictionary, particularly when it is clear and simple and has as few syntactic problems as Borges's poetry, which I find relatively easy. I did a number of poems because Norman Thomas di Giovanni approached me, and this all centered on one poem.

Did I tell you that anecdote? It's a little spooky. It's essentially a Borgesian anecdote. About 1968 di Giovanni said that he'd been thinking of various people to assign particular Borges poems to, and he thought that I might like to do the poem about the golem. I was startled at this because my mother's family traditionally believes that my mother's father's family is descended from the Rabbi of Prague about whom the golem stories have circulated. Without telling di Giovanni anything about this, I said, "Yes, all right, I will do the poem."[7] I followed the original meter and rhyme scheme, and the syntax of the poem made it quite easy to do. I could preserve the rhyme of *Golem* and *Gershom Scholem*, who is the great commentator on Cabalism—that's a very Borgesian rhyme, rhyming a myth with its exegete—and I could hold those things over from the original, and it worked out rather well. When the work was over I did want Borges to know that there had been a kind of loop in time. In the same meter of the translation I wrote him a verse letter about having done this, and about the curious historical accident, and everything else.

EH   When did you do this—in 1968?

JH   Yes. I was in England at the time. This verse letter to Borges I remember starting, "I've never been to Prague, and the last time that I was there, its stones sang in the rain. . . ."

EH   That's interesting. Here's your translation of the Borges poem on the golem [*indicating it in the anthology*]. I've read it in Spanish but didn't look at your translation. You said you followed the original meter. I remember it as being almost prose. In Spanish there's usually only syllabic count. Did you find accentual meter?

JH   Yes, in rhymed quatrains.

EH   I mean linear meter.

JH   It's a kind of pentameter.

EH   [*quoting the first stanza*] "Si (como el griego en el Cratilo) / El nombre es arquetipo de la cosa, / En la letras de rosa está la rosa / Y todo el Nilo en la palabra Nilo."

JH   Would you say that's according to a syllabic count?

EH   Well, it seems hendecasyllabic, and also like mixed meters. At any rate, it's rare to find pentameter in the Spanish. One of the things about Borges is that I think he wants to be an English poet.

JH   Oh, without question. But he frequently does that in the sonnets. He moves toward a pentameter.

EH   O.K. Another question I have for you is really three questions in one. Where or when does the translator, or the translation itself, begin? How does the translation develop? And where does it end? The implication is that the poetic translation doesn't start when you put your pencil to paper, but before that. What do you think?

JH   It would start with a sense of what shape, what form, the finished product is going to have. One of the confusing things about this matter in the modernist tradition is that the poem format for English that Pound virtually invented looks as if it were a prose paragraph. That is, a kind of Poundian free verse in end-stopped lines he used for the Chinese poems, for example. And so one has to be aware of that as an alternative and a possibility too. There has to be some notion of how the shape is to be carried over or what it is to be carried over into. That is, when you've finished, what it will be and what it will look like. I'm not saying a verse form necessarily precedes the translation, but something like it does—an

overall sense of form which may have surfaced, with clear surface man-
ifestations. Or it may be a deeper, more abstract sense of form. You
could say, "Well, I know this is written in complicated stanza structures,
but I'm going to do it in one blob because there is something that I want
to get out of it that is best represented by that." That's a formal idea, just
as with writing a poem something happens like that. By which I suppose
I mean that doing a translation is very like doing a poem.

EH   Right. I'd imagine you'd think so. I want to know about one particular area now. You spoke of translating sonnets, and you thought of
the job as that of writing an equivalent or correspondent sonnet.

JH   Well, that was because it was Borges, and because of what the form
meant to him, I thought it important to get that relation to the English
sonnet into my translation, although I could certainly conceive of translating some other poet's sonnet in another language and not trying to
keep that form. On principle I don't think one should trash the poem. It's
the problem of finding a viable analogue, and in so many traditions there
are viable analogues. There's one of putting French into English, and
that tradition involves substituting pentameters for the alexandrines.
Now any translation of a contemporary French poem that doesn't have
anything palpable to do with earlier French formal conventions, nevertheless still has to draw on the history of that relationship, and this is the
difference between a good and a not-so-good translation. In some languages there are no traditions at all of bringing things over, in which case
the problem is a very different one.

EH   That's a good point.

JH   Translating from some languages into English, even though they
have a long literary tradition, might well be the same as translating from
a textless language. And translating from a textless language is a totally
different process, I would think. It now seems very popular among a lot
of people who despise textuality and despise tradition.

EH   You mean as from American Indian languages?

JH   Yes.

EH   A lot of that is being done nowadays.

JH   Yes, it's being done—done by people who don't know the languages at all.

EH   Mostly, yes.

JH And it's a very safe kind of hackwork. Also its ideological content is sufficiently belligerent to give the piece an edge. There's something politically ideological about translating American Indian poetry, and that sort of thing. I don't mean the very careful versions done for the Department of the Interior or the Bureau of Indian Affairs.

EH I understand the Smithsonian Institution Reports or Transactions usually serve as a base for many of the translations of Indian poetry.

JH Yes, and I'm thinking of the whole idea of versifying them. They are versified into the flagrant gestures of what are called naked forms, I believe, by some of the practitioners, which simply means the received style of the moment. Professor Harold Bloom of Yale compares W. S. Merwin to Longfellow interestingly with respect to two notions. One is that both of them based a large part of their work on translations. And, secondly, that both wrote—that is, helped create and then wrote—in what was the received style of their time. If you look at magazine verse from the 1860s and 1870s in America, in *Godey's Ladies' Book*, *Peterson's Magazine*, and that sort of thing, all of it will be imitation Longfellow. And, similarly, if you look at poetry magazines today, a lot of it is imitation Merwin. Now the relation of that to translation I think is very interesting. You see: I think Longfellow's *Hiawatha* is an example of just the thing we're talking about. It's taken to be "Indian" but based on the Kalevala. Yet the meter comes not from the Kalevala, which Longfellow couldn't read—he didn't know a word of Finnish; it comes from a German translation which converts the octosyllabics of the Finnish into trochaic tetrameter, a pounding meter in German. You know the one that Heine used unrhymed for so many poems. That's where the heavy beat comes from, because in the Finnish you can't really say it's trochaics. . . .

EH What kind of meter would you call *Hiawatha*?

JH Trochaic tetrameter unrhymed.

EH You know, it now occurs to me that you're also speaking of the meter of Pound's first Canto: "and then went down to the ships. . . ."

JH Well, there, in the first Canto, Pound is playing. Originally a lot more of it was iambic pentameter. In the original draft of that canto it's almost pure Browning. Then Pound jumped back and developed the notion but just in the first Canto as we now have it, or particularly there—the notion that there was an analogue for him in the two parts of the possible hexameter line, separated by a caesura, and the two parts of the German line, the Germanic four-stressed line, separated by the scholar's artificial line-break in the text. You know he'd been interested in the relation between visual format and a structural marker very early, which is why he takes Cavalcanti's *endecasillabo* line and writes it on the page in three successive lines, each one three successive line thirds—each one shoved over one step to the right so as to give you the three lifts.

EH   It's a line divided into three distinct parts.

JH   That's right. But descending. Written in three lines descending toward the right.

EH   It's what Williams does.

JH   Well, Williams probably copied that variable-foot format from Pound's earlier use, except that what Williams says about the variable foot is sheer garbage. It doesn't make any sense. What Pound did was to see that relation. It would be a little bit like taking the first line of Dante's *Inferno* and writing it as three lines: "Nel mezzo / del cammin / di nostra vita," which would show the three lifts of the Italian hendecasyllabic line. He did that with a couple of Dante things, and so got interested in the original format. What he finally came to was a meter that is the six cut in half that way, stacked this way, sometimes echoing against the four-stressed line—and then every once in a while he'll have an absolutely pure hexameter come out. "Ear, ear for the sea surge. Murmur of old men's voices"—which is an accentual Homeric line.

EH   O.K. I'd like to go back to that psychological matter of where the translation begins and how it proceeds and ends. Obviously it's different each time. Do you have anything to say about the experience—commissions aside now—of deciding to do a poem out of love, for its author or for the thing itself?

JH   That's interesting. In going on with you about translating, I've been talking about some rather formal, commissioned translating. In some of my recent poems I have embedded translations. But those are thefts, as it were, not formal translations. For example, I have a poem in my last book which is an expansion—I simply call it "After Callimachus." It's an expansion of an epigram of Callimachus but it's been changed—it's put into a different metrical frame. Some of the imagery is changed and expanded. It's an imitation, just the way a lot of seventeenth-century English poems are imitations of Catullus, not strict

ones by any means. But that sort of thing started out naturally and differently because it wasn't done with the task of translating in mind. It was
just preserving something. And I have done this with bits and passages of
poetry in the past—just put them in. Well, for example, I once did a half-
translation, half mistranslation-adaptation of a great little poem of
Hölderlin's.

EH   How did that start?

JH   That started simply by my wanting to get inside the Hölderlin
poem, which I've known a good part of my literate life.

EH   But you'd never translated it?

JH   No, I'd never translated it. And to begin with, I found myself playing with a mistranslation of it. In my version, the third line is not a literal
translation of the German, it's a mistranslation, which produces a new
image. I'm interested in that. And so I translated some of it, then in the
middle wrote about five lines, completely mine but just generated by the
translation, then continued by closing off the translation. I used the piece
as the dedicatory poem of my book, *The Night Mirror*. But when it was
published in the *Partisan Review*, without any identification, an angry letter came in from somebody claiming that I had stolen it from Hölderlin,
which amused me, because it's one of the most famous poems in German. I suppose I've done this sort of thing a few times.

EH   We're talking in some way about the old idea that all writing is
a kind of collaboration. And maybe now it's time the sterile polemics and
argumentation induced by the question of being faithful to the original is
countered by showing that one form of faithfulness is a matter of doing
a new work.

JH   In some cases a great new work comes from a terribly faithful
translation. I can think of one in English where a great English poem in
translation is made of a great Italian poem. And that is Rossetti's translation of Dante's "Stony Sestina." Just a plain masterpiece. It's one of the
greatest English poems of the nineteenth century, and very accurate as
a translation.

EH   Nineteenth-century translators of that stature—Rossetti, Longfellow, FitzGerald—actually had a great deal more on the ball than most
twentieth-century English and American translators.

JH   Oh, I think so. Rossetti, particularly in that very very great poem.
It's because of what the poem's about. I mean it's for all the right rea-

sons—one of those sestinas in which the terminal words make up a poem in themselves: *ombra, colli, erba, verde, pietra, donna* (*shade, hills, grass, green, stone, lady*), and really give you a distillation of the poem, and he could keep those and work with them. The Rossetti poem is not certainly the most allegorized reading of Dante, but an unallegorized reading of the poem would be the obsessive one for Rossetti in his own imaginative, erotic mythology, and it was an absolutely perfect thing for him to do and he did it magnificently. I have used some lines from that poem and some lines from Pound—and, mind you, the Rossetti was done in the 1850s or 1860s. I gave both to students without identifying the poems and said one is by a pre-Raphaelite poet, the other is by Ezra Pound, who believed in precision.

EH   That's a good trick!

JH   And naturally they all assumed that Rossetti was the real poet, and the Pound manner limping, lumpy, fussy.

EH   I want to ask you more about the question of a unified theory of translation, a theory that would accord with the practice of translators and present an imaginative confrontation of the possibilities. What you were telling me about your own practice is very close. . . .

JH   Well, the theory of translation would have to be a theory of literature in general.

EH   Yes, all right.

JH   And I think this is a point that Adams[8] gets to and a point that Steiner[9] doesn't get to in his, for me, disappointing book.

EH   Well, Steiner in his second chapter, I think, is more imaginative. At any rate, one of those early chapters goes into the question of the mystic notion of language having originated in the first word of God. The attractive thing there is that the idea allows for the work of translation to be considered as much an original as the primary text is, where both are striving to achieve something like the lost but reconstituted word.

JH   Yes, but I much prefer to read Milton on that subject: the invocation to Book One or Three of *Paradise Lost* goes into that.

EH   You have a point.

JH   I think all one can do in surveys of that kind is to look at what translations have actually been done by which people under what circumstances for what purposes, and generalize from that. I think that's very interesting. For example, I think you could give in fairly concrete linguistic terms some of the reasons why for an English speaker the Douay Bible in French sounds silly. One thing Steiner doesn't go into which is absolutely essential to literary translation, is the whole question of what the Germans call *Sprachgefühl*, the language sense you have. What is it about speaking English that makes you think. . . . Well, put it this way: I say to graduate students, "I want to give you some English monosyllables and I want you to tell me whether they're French or Germanic in origin," and I give them a list including the word *push*. Without thinking, they might say, "Well, that's German." But of course it isn't.

EH   *Push?*

JH   Yes. But they assume it's German for good reason. It's part of the *Sprachgefühl* of English.

EH   So Steiner does not. . . .

JH   Wait, just a second. So *Sprachgefühl* is very important for things of this kind. Lichtenberg has a great aphorism. He says, "A donkey is a horse translated into Dutch." Now, that is funny if you're a speaker of (a) German or (b) English. Otherwise it isn't funny, because Dutch is for speakers of both English and German something like a recognizable but too highly distorted version of their language.

EH   Yes.

JH   Dutch is midway between German and English in that respect, so that the relation between correct *horse* and bungled *donkey* is like the relation: correct English or German, bungled Dutch. You see. Now matters of this sort are very interesting. They would lead one in English to say, "Oh, the Douay Bible, I'll just pick a passage from the Old Testament and read it in French and it sounds funny. It sounds as if it weren't serious." These are interesting linguistic questions, but ones that Steiner doesn't go in for.

I think that certain canonical translations in the history of certain languages and literature have a great shaping force. The English Bible has had effects on the structure of English poetry that have *nothing* to do with doctrine. For example, if I were trying to write a book on translation (and I would not attempt to do so) one thing I would comment on would be this—a simple tiny matter, but with vast consequences for English poetry. The King James translators handled a particular Hebrew syntactic problem in one way rather than another: the so-called Hebrew construct-state, which puts two nouns in a certain relation to each other.

Hebrew is uninflected, but the two nouns are put together in a combinatorial way, and it's not a specifically genitive relationship, so that for example: literally in Hebrew you say "house of the book," for *school*; it should be translated in the German or Greek mode of English as "book-house," and it has that sense of book house. It does not have the genitive sense of "books' house," you see. Nevertheless, we have another option for combination in English from the Germanic or the Greek, which are the same, and that is the French, the romance tradition, which is to make a phrase out of it, "house of the book." Now that "of the" is very ambiguous in English. It could be a genitive construction or it could be a partitive one, and the King James translators, using that partitive construction throughout, thus generate implicit allegorizations and personifications. Take the phrase "the house of the book." It is a house in which the book dwells, it is the house that belongs to the book, it is the house infused with the book, it is the house which is itself a trope for the book. You see?

EH   Right.

JH   Whenever you have those constructions in the King James Bible, then you have a part allegorization. It's what gives the Bible its poetic richness all the time and is a basic building block of English poetic vocabulary; so that when you end up with a phrase, a resonant phrase in Wallace Stevens, say, like "the malady of the quotidian," you ask, "Well, what does that mean? Does it mean the *fact* that there's a quotidian which is in itself a malady? Or, does it mean that the quotidian brings particular maladies of its own with it?" And of course it means both, and of course Stevens is playing on that resonant ambivalence of the construction that is traceable to the Bible.

EH   Yes. Well, by saying that, you're also implying what you said before—that to have a unified theory of translation means nothing more or less than a theory of literature.

JH   It "means nothing more or less"? No. Put it this way: a theory of literature is a necessary, perhaps insufficient, condition for a theory of translation, but I think a theory of translation is part of the theory of literature.

EH   But in the example from the King James Bible, you're also talking about the style, the literary style, of English verse and its products into our own time.

JH   No. I would go on to talk about the literary style of English verse by saying that a construction, "house of the book," rather than "the book-house," lends itself more to accentual syllabic verse, to regular iambic verse, with few inversions, than does the Germanic-Greek re-compounding, which gives you a lot more spondees.

EH All right.

JH And you'll notice that as new words come into English—say with the Industrial Revolution—you get a lot more words that will be spelled with hyphens and that will be spondaic, because they will be that kind of compound. Mr. Fulton invented a steamboat, which was stressed búnk-búnk (like names, Jóhn Smíth)—*steámboát*. Those compounds tend to show the boundaries of the iambic alteration. One of the things that happens, of course, is that when *steamboat* eventually gets to be an accepted compound, the secondary stress is removed, and it becomes stressed on the first syllable. That's how you know the compound has become a thing, and say *steám*boat.

EH Do you think that for the theorist of translation there is something to be gained from a study of linguistics? I know you have been a student of linguistics.

JH No, I'm not, though I've learned a little about it.

EH Well, I was thinking of transformational theories, like Chomsky's. Steiner thinks that he has to answer or contend with Chomsky. How do you feel about that?

JH I'd rather not talk about Steiner and Chomsky because Chomsky has made clear what he feels about Steiner's understanding of his work.

EH All right.

JH I think linguistics is very important. I don't necessarily mean that one particular mode of analysis of one set of problems in one philosophical context is what linguistics is. Since I'm not a linguist, I'm free not to have to worry about what the boundaries of the subject are. I think historical grammar is very important: knowledge of the structures of language, knowledge of the relations between grammatical change and semantic change are very important, and the relations that those things have to trope are very important. I mean, I do think that we should know—because it's part of the life of poetry to deal with this—something about how, when the Indo-European languages began to be studied, one inevitable conclusion was that there had originally been a small stock of words, and that these had numerically expanded by processes of trope. That's certainly a very nineteenth-century theory; it looks most like biological recapitulation—that is, that in the ontogeny of a particular bit of synchronic metaphor, the phylogeny of the history of the language has been recapitulated, et cetera, et cetera. Well, I think that these matters are certainly important, yes.

Look, Milton uses a phenomenon of etymology as a very important figure throughout *Paradise Lost*. The relation between the primary quality of the meaning of a word that we ordinarily use and an antithetical kind of primary quality, that of its prior etymological meaning, and how these come up against each other, are for him a basic metaphor of the then and the now, of the fallen and the unfallen.

EH Right, exactly. So one can say with Milton, without being Milton, that there's a way of approaching the subject of translation in terms of an imaginative adaptation of theories of literature, in the general sense, and particular linguistic theories.

JH Yes, I think the truest poetry is the most feigning, and probably the most satisfactory and effective translations will have the virtue of being appropriate to their literary and historical milieus. A certain kind of accuracy—one of definition, one sense of what accuracy means—has been appropriate to certain aspects of modernism, but there are great loose, free, adaptive translations. Compare Ben Jonson's and Campion's versions of the Catullus poem, the "vivamus mea Lesbia atque amemus," which do totally different things with it. I mean, Campion translates the first few lines, comes to the line, "the ever-during night" (the "nox est perpetua una dormienda"), "the one ever-during night," has that as his line, and loves it so much that he takes it as a refrain, and builds a new poem in two successive strophes; using that as a refrain, he leaves Catullus and writes a wonderful little poem of his own that ends up with that fine image of "When I die I want people to be screwing on my tomb," et cetera. He gets to it by starting from Catullus, and then taking off, having seen the resonance of one particular line. Ben Jonson moves right through it and does something else. However, you have these two great Catullan versions, and that's an age, of course, in which people dwelled so much with classical texts that they could do what they wanted with them. In one sense, to let somebody know what Martial is really like, I would send him not to any particular translations of Martial but to J. V. Cunningham's *Epigrams*, even ones that aren't direct. Cunningham has translated some of Martial, but some of his own original ones are absolutely *it*. They're the best ever, the best resuscitations of that kind of thing ever done.

EH Well, you seem to be saying in another way something that we started with: namely, that much of the activity of translation is implicit in learning how to produce poems, and doing that is a completely self-educating process.

JH Oh, yes, absolutely.

EH You mentioned Campion and Jonson's reworkings of Catullus. That's one example.

JH Look, in English the experimental aspect of the problem starts not with Chaucer getting French into English, but with Wyatt trying to get Petrarch into English and not knowing how. It really starts there with that kind of experiment, and then is repeated again and again in the history of English poetry. Sidney doing it, getting into Petrarch successfully. . . .

EH You mean by getting into Petrarch, the sonnet?

JH I'm talking about the form and the diction of the sonnet.

EH What about the subject?

JH Well, the first getting of the subject into English occurs in *Troilus and Criseyde*. There is an inset bit, which is actually a translation of one of the Petrarch *rime* there. But it didn't have consequences of that kind; it wasn't the same thing. It wasn't Petrarchan, but the first Petrarchan attempt till Sidney, and then Surrey solves the problem immediately thereafter, and gets it right, and with his good ear manages to decide that the iambic pentameter line is the one to do the hendecasyllable in, although Wyatt tried every possible kind of thing as a way to do it. I mean, those poems are truly experimental and Wyatt possibly didn't know what he was doing.

But this problem, whether it's one kind of technical problem at one level or another, is really at the heart of the matter and keeps going through. Tennyson has so much of the Greek and Latin poetry that it just keeps flowing out all the time, and so many poets as different as Dryden and Tennyson have in common, say, the Vergil in their heads. When Dryden writes that beautiful elegy to John Oldham and when he ends up with that beautiful line, "Then night and gloomy death encompass thee around," he is doing a free translation of a line in the Sixth Book of the *Aeneid* that he himself translates a little more accurately and tightly in another place when he actually does the Vergil. But he feels free simply to do that, whether it is—as the late Ben Brower said—whether in Pope it is a poetry of allusion, allusion as a kind of trope in itself, or whether it is simply there; it is built into the language. Now, does one call that formal translation, that kind of allusion, or not, or what?

EH   Well, you're talking about the business of the poet, I suppose.

JH   I think that's always there, and I think as Adams pointed out there is such a thing as translating from earlier phases of English into our own.

EH   Yes.

JH   And I don't mean just Pope's formal redoings of Donne's *Satires*, and things like that, you see. I mean simply keeping the continuity of the language going.

EH   Yes. One common device is to ask students to translate Shakespeare into modern verse without knowing whether in the beginning they know anything about Shakespeare or much about modern verse. Assuming they knew a little about both, they would then begin to see that there's a problem, or what the problems are. Then, also, you feel that certain crucial texts to illustrate changes in style, or the inauguration of a new style, would be necessary to solidify the translation, as in the Bible?

JH   Yes, I think the Bible is very interesting in that aspect.

EH   Well, we've reached high noon. Thanks very much.

JH   Right, my pleasure.

3 / Herbert Mason

EH   I'm going to begin by putting one or two questions to you about translation. First, what started you translating? What interests lay behind your doing what you did?

HM   We're speaking of the *Gilgamesh*, a verse narrative that I wrote some years ago. In that book[10] an autobiographical postscript tells how I learned about the story of Gilgamesh and how I approached it. I did *not* do it as a translator on first learning about the materials through Professor Albert Lord at Harvard. I thought of the work in a very personal sense. I had known the experience of grief through my father's death when I was very young and then, about the same time as I was learning *Gilgamesh*, a very close friend at Harvard got Hodgkin's disease and was to die soon afterward. So that the poem for me became an inner tale that made sense of the confusion caused by loss, the metaphysical worry, the pain, in the face of these experiences. I really thought of it as an epic poem that I wanted to write. I didn't think of it, and still don't, as a translation.

As time went on I tried writing various versions of it, and these versions, which I still have, I don't want ever to go back to. But as I recall them they reflect the literary influences of that time. Gradually I sort of outran those influences, or my use or misuse of them, and simply came to terms with the story itself—less with my own subjective losses and so on, and more with the elements of the story and the desire to put them together in a unified way by concentrating on the themes of friendship and loss and quest. In other words, I lived with the fragments of the tale for many years. I think Pasternak talked about translators needing to live with a work (in this case, a story) for a long time before actually beginning to do something about it.

Then a series of convergences occurred. One was a trip I took to the Near East during which I stopped in Paris and told this story to a painter friend of mine. I should say that all those years I always *told* the story like a sort of Ancient Mariner, his inner heart, as it were.

EH May I interrupt you a moment? The story you're now telling is about how you wanted to rewrite *Gilgamesh*, or is it about what you had decided, after reading it, that you could write? What I'm trying to get at is (and this concerns a question we might get to later about what it is one actually translates): Was there such a thing for you as an *absent* text?

HM Right. Well, I had to deal with this. As time went on, and as I saw *Gilgamesh* through the eyes of other people—particularly my painter friend—I got different ideas as to what was most effective in the retelling. It was not, I found out, a retelling in modern dress, or a rendering of it in clothes that would be contemporary or relevant, and so on. What affected other people was the sense of the story's originality, an oldness and yet timelessness, you see. So I began in the late sixties to get more and more concerned about the text, the original text, and more desirous of knowing it.

I don't know if this is a digression, but perhaps I need it to explain what happened. I had thought at one time of going back to Harvard as a graduate student in Akkadian, so that I could begin a scholarly study of *Gilgamesh* and have some sense of the original. However, through my years abroad, living in France and studying with Louis Massignon, I became very intrigued by the Near East but especially the medieval world and the world of Islam. And so when I did go back to Harvard, I went into Arabic and Persian, with some other projects in mind that ran parallel to *Gilgamesh*. So *Gilgamesh* became more of a personal story, combined with a reverence for the text, an increasing desire to know the text. I really had to come to terms with the text through translations in English, German, and French, but with some sense of its linguistic structure, although not the *sounds*, which are an important difference. Now the problem is really that we don't have a text for *Gilgamesh* and the most coherent and unified version of those tales is the Babylonian version which was discovered in the nineteenth century in Nineveh, in temple ruins there. Over the years I have fastened on the Babylonian version, but I have concentrated my own thought on the same themes that I began

with: loss and the confrontation with one's own mortality and the quest
for immortality or, as in this poem, the acceptance of mortality. But I
began to adhere more and more to what I could get hold of in the original
fragments and try to add to that, through metaphors and similes and epic
devices that I had learned in my study of narrative and epic poetry.

EH Your case—which in some ways is very unusual because you came
to the work indirectly and then learned what existed of the text afterwards—confirms what I have often felt is essential: that the translator
have a very special relationship to the text, particularly a personal relationship. And I now have a question about the text: Is the text you confront a stable quantity, first of all, and then, in practice, a variable
quality? This question has to do with what happens when you confront
the text itself. Is it something physical when you begin, that makes you
translate word by word, phrase by phrase, and then something that
changes as you translate, so that in fact you begin to produce a version, in
the way you speak of it, which becomes part and parcel of the text, whatever the text turns out to be?

HM Well, it's hard for me in a sense. Let me say only that the architecture of the story is made stable by steady and careful concentration on
specific themes within it. This ties the episodic parts together into a
whole, though not necessarily the Babylonian whole and certainly not
the original Sumerian. But let me say also that I don't see myself as
a translator of *Gilgamesh*; that's the difficult thing. The text is with me,
although I feel that I have a sense of the original text, but it's by way of
identifying my own intuition and my own self, feeling, and experience
with the originals of the text, the original figures of the text.

EH Well, you went back. . . .

HM I went back into the worldview and into that symbolism and
imagery and such, as one goes back into a cave, and is amazed at exploring all that is in the cave, to discover a sensation of timelessness there.

EH Yes, you've mentioned that. You said that in talking to people over
the years you found that what interested them was the timeless and original quality of the epic, and I think your translation-adaptation succeeds
so well because it brings that out in a very immediate, simple, and powerful way. Though you don't call it a translation, and though it's been
called an adaptation, it isn't written in the language that you would
normally use in writing your poetry, for example.

HM   No, that's true. But my own *poétique* is stimulated increasingly by narrative and dramatic situation and character and by concentration on the whole worldview underlying my fragments of experience. I aspire to simplicity of language for the evocation of plot and people, which is why I'm also drawn to poetic fiction. I seek my own most evocative voice in the context and form attracting me. I think that *Gilgamesh* overtook me somewhat and made me write with a greater simplicity and clarity than I would have, or than I did in fact aspire to in earlier versions. At a certain point, as I say, some things converged that made *me* surrender to the text of the story or plot, as it were, and its uncovered form dictated a language. What happened to me afterwards, you know, was that I *did* become a translator, but of other things. I had to earn my living at one point by translating a large work of scholarship in French and Arabic into English, and that had a similar effect on me in this sense. I became a translator, in the formal sense of that word—the job also required editing on my part, of a two-thousand-page work. But the materials, the substance of that work, began to overtake *me* and then I made another evocation, as I would call it, of the subject of this work.

EH   What is the title of the work?

HM   The title is *The Passion of Al-Hallaj* by Louis Massignon. After doing two and a half volumes of the work, sponsored by the Bollingen Foundation Series, I began to be overwhelmed as I had been by *Gilgamesh*, and so I tried to find out what my voice was in this material—not just the translator's role, but *my* voice. I wanted to write *my* Hallaj, because I identified personally with him. So I wrote another dramatic narrative. In this instance I could control the original poems of Hallaj, which were of themselves "stable," as you say, but which became variable in terms of voice by my surrender and mixture with their voice. Their tone and spiritual authenticity, intimate and conversational with God, are what in style impressed me most; I had also translated some of his odes from tenth-century Arabic, and I've since published those.

EH   Where are they?

HM   They're in the *Anthology of Arabic Literature*, published by Twayne. I wanted most to dramatize Hallaj's life and death in his character—bring him out as a real person to me and to others—using some of his work or imitating some of the tone and character of his work, in my own language and sense of structure, of a narrative poem. And I did this in one winter. It actually happened two winters ago, and again it was written in conjunction with another person, in part. Where in *Gilgamesh* the painter had affected me, here an actor affected me very much and as I wrote, he and I would read some of it, and so it became a play, as it were. We've given it a few times now in concert readings at universities. I don't consider that a translation but it is based on translation; it is my own process of translation. I feel that translation is a process of gaining intimacy with a work, or a person, or another mode of expression, or another time.

EH But your identifying the character of voice is also interesting, because good translations are works that make one believe in the authenticity of a voice, even if it's somewhat strange. Willard Trask said that his having been an actor was an aspect of his life that helped his work—perhaps the ability to project a voice, quite literally. You seem to be saying something of that sort.

HM I'm a more private person than Willard in that sense, so that I may have to work doubly hard to get out of myself and project a voice. What *I* have found is that I work very well with another person. I have to get a sense of the other person that I'm dealing with, be it Gilgamesh or Hallaj or. . . . I've done some other things on some Alexander legends and such. I have to get a sense of the character, and very often it's a friend or somebody else coming from another discipline, another art, who can give me a handle on that art and project me, because my work is very . . . kind of inward and meditative, perhaps to a fault. It's a little too narrative in that sense, and just now, where, as I told you before, I'm writing fiction and plays actually, I may end up where Willard began. It's been a process of dragging me out of myself into the open, into a sense of audience, and I think that has happened now.

EH That's interesting. This summer I discovered through a friend that Martin Buber had been a theater buff in his youth and never missed a play; he haunted theaters from adolescence on. I was thinking of your interest in religion in this connection. One hears a voice or wants to hear a voice and that's just what leads one to go on.

HM I do believe in the Muse, the Daemon. I think that one is driven by the sense of something beyond oneself that is speaking. I thoroughly believe in that. Whether you call it religion or religious, I don't know. I suspend judgment on that for a while. Reality is plausible, you know, if not always desirable. Let's say that there is a reality there because there is something other than the reality of one's self; and that there is another that draws it out ultimately beyond our necessary awareness of ambiguities and beyond ambiguity itself; and my illustrating it through these other people who have drawn it out is part of the phenomenon and process of surrender and evocation. But then there's some sense of a calling, of something, and it *is* a voice, a voice that speaks unlike an echo, and uses the talents you've been preparing and so on. I will say another thing here—that I don't consider myself a lyric person, but a narrative person, in the formal and perhaps also the spiritual sense.

EH Narrative *and* epic.

HM Narrative and epic. For a number of years I misconstrued myself as a lyric person and I tried to work through short poems of my own, some of which I published, most of which are ghastly, because they're too strained. I couldn't use the sense of structure that I had in that particular way. So the discovery of *Gilgamesh* was for me a release in part to the *form* that I have. I consider myself basically a transmitter of stories—if I were defining what I am. I got that from a student who in one class where we were dealing with translation a lot, and myth and various things of the sort, said to me, "How do you define yourself?" And I said, "I don't know." And he said, "I know. You're a transmitter of stories."

EH When you say you believe in the Muse and you say you follow what you hear, then you are an intermediary in some way. I have a feeling that's true of all creative work. One hears something, one tries to listen to it, make it out, then in doing so one begins to speak in the voice one hears. Well, I seem to believe in the Muse too.

HM The Muse speaks to me or calls me to do sort of large works which are strange for our day perhaps, but I seem to be able to operate only in a large story form, and use lyricism in that. In fact, the lyricism occurs for me only within the framework of a narrative epic poem or a drama. I have written some sonnets, but I'm letting them sit for a bit because they work only insofar as they form a sequence with an overall structure. I think individually they don't.

EH Well, from all you've been saying, it seems you wouldn't then be the sort of person to ask about the differences between translation involving a transformation of the text and the other, which is a sort of shadowing of the text, because it's clear that all you've done is a transformation.

HM Well, but there are stages in that process. I mean, I will speak to that in this way. I think that in the odes of Hallaj, which are longish poems, not just lyric poems, I have to go through various stages of a literal translation, in a sense an imitation—then an interpretive translation. I really think there are values in each of these stages, but the only one that makes sense, in terms of a complete book to be presented to students, is that of an interpretive "shadowing" translation, one presumed to achieve some sense of the immediacy and reality of the voice while adding our other knowledge, you see. I mean, the knowledge of the times, the arts and perspectives, the various things finding their way into the timbre of the voice. So we interpret it. We interpret meanings into our own language, and when a certain thing is said in a particular way we have to translate ourselves first into the world in which it was said while knowing that in our own world we say the same thing with different words. Then we have to create metaphors, where there weren't any sometimes, because only with a metaphor can we achieve the effect they do, let's say, with a theological statement, which is abstract. So anyone insisting on the purity of the text when looking at the translation wants something else than a living translation or evocation. I'm not happily disposed to doing just that sort of work, except as a part of the process of getting translated into the work.

EH Which makes sense, and goes back to what you said earlier about letting *Gilgamesh* mature with you and opening the idea to others (which brought in their persons, their characters), and then letting the world fill out, through your experience, what you were going to write. You quoted Pasternak about the length of time it takes to do a solid translation. So it also seems that you were stage-managing, if it can be put that way, the act of eventually doing this work—which is to say that you were using a dramatic form.

HM You know when you invited me down to Brown last year to read—and yesterday I gave another reading of *Gilgamesh* here in Boston—in going through it that way I sense where the original is. I have a sense of the spine of the story and a few of the formulas, the epic formulas, used in the original. Also, I note where I've added to it through metaphor and simile, and certain images used to make it a little more timeless, to set it for other people at any other place, at any time, but also particular places that they can respond to. So when I *hear* what I've done with the thing, I know its limitations as a scholarly translation and its strengths as a poem. But something else has happened to me since the poem was published: that is, it's grown further with me beyond the printed stage. I used to tell the story orally, without a text of my own or anybody else's, to classes and one or two audiences, before it was published, and I found the variations in that telling to be very revealing. I had begun to use certain formulas myself in order to station it, along through its structure, but would embellish it in various ways. Now *that's* the problem, right there, with an ancient text: that there isn't a "text" nor supposed to be a "text." There's an inherited structure we get—and I regarded myself simply as one of the tellers of *Gilgamesh*. It has variations in the telling, and I have told it many times. Now some of the tellings, as in the case of Homer, have come down to us and we have those particular tellings, but to pretend to have a true text is to miss the point of the whole process of oral narration. What I published was simply one set of variations on the telling that I had done over the years. Maybe I should have said that in the beginning, to clarify this whole matter.

EH   Well, your explanation makes a lot of sense now. It lights up what you were saying earlier. The poem exists off the page as an oral presentation, or epic, and that's just what an epic is—a story that's spoken.

HM   Right—and as I read it (I take the book with me and read it), as I do even now, I have further variations, because I sort of digress. I come to a point and then add something that isn't on the printed page.

EH   Do these amount to substantial additions?

HM   Well, I'm really looking ahead to a new edition of that book, and I've written down marginally some of the additions I remember. I'd also like some of the paintings by my friend to illustrate the new edition. Because a new process has occurred. As it were, I have been fighting the text that I've printed, so as not to be confined by it. That's another dimension to the whole thing. I really think this story is with me forever, for better or worse.

EH   It's appropriated you.

HM   It has appropriated me and I simply retell it many ways and many times, but I always come back to its inherent structure and not to a text. I don't think the text is the crucial thing. I think once you have learned, almost memorized, the building blocks, the progress of the poem, you can go off without anything in hand—pen or pencil—and I can see why then you could be a blind poet. All you need then is the inner imagery, the imagination at work, the structures basically set in place, and a certain number of formulas that you use yourself. Sometimes, of course, in our age, we use themes as the ancients did, sometimes just in a line that captures a thing and recurs throughout the poem. I think an epic poem, particularly one like *Gilgamesh*, has a very small vocabulary, a very small set of themes which recur in variations over and over so that there are patterns and sinews that run through and intertwine and tighten the whole work.

EH   A constant reinforcement of things.

HM   A reinforcement.

EH   And then one can see how that would be close to the condition of music, the song accompanying epic telling.

HM   Yes.

EH   Are we getting close to the time when you must leave?

HM   Yes, I'm afraid so.

EH   Then perhaps we'll come back. Goodbye for now, and thanks.

Laurence J. Hyman

4 / Ben Belitt

EH   Ben, I'd like to begin by asking how you started translating, since the experience of each translator is rather different. In the case of some poets like John Hollander, translation came as a kind of apprenticeship to the writing of poetry; it was the "grammar" for his own poetic development.

BB   I would agree that translation is a kind of jungle gym for the exercise of all the faculties and muscles required for the practice of poetry, even if it doesn't always begin that way—that it serves the calisthenic function of bringing to bear upon what is translated one's total resources and cunning as a poet. In this sense, translation takes translators far beyond the genre of their own recognizable styles and idiosyncrasies as poets. One of the disintegrative benefits of translation is that it compels or seduces one into writing poetry other than one's own. . . .

I suppose my own experience with translation first came as a by-product of my close reading of the French symbolist poets with Wallace Fowlie at Bennington, as a kind of unofficial seminar for aging amateurs exclusively invented for my benefit between 1937 and 1940. It was the idiom of Rimbaud, I remember, which excited and gratified me most at the time. My knowledge of French was such that, although I could imagine what the tension and weight of the idiom was in French, I couldn't get close enough to the sound and excitement of it without touching it with English and, as Keats says, "proving it on my own pulses."

EH   So you started with Rimbaud as a poet whose language and style were very sympathetic.

BB More than sympathetic. I felt an invisible opening for myself, somewhere under the French, as a poet in search of a language that *mattered*. I was looking for accelerations, truncations, oddity, energy, character—everything one associates with the high tensions and syntactical speeds of Rimbaud. All the poems turned into "personal versions" the moment I touched them with a little English as a kind of venture in private acoustics. I wanted to "score" Rimbaud in a way that was identical with my own *hearing*, rather than constantly making allowances for correspondences I was told should exist for all sensitive Frenchmen: I longed for the immediacy of poetry in English while still parsing the French and computing alexandrines.

I set about "translating" Rimbaud as a greedy amateur for my own instruction and pleasure because I was imprudently (or helplessly) drawn to the four ambitious set pieces—"Le Bateau ivre," "Les Premières Communions," "Mémoire," "Les Poètes de sept ans"—that I later published in a small volume in this country and in England as *Four Poems by Rimbaud: The Problem of Translation*. The title was a later deception of the English publisher, which promised more than it delivered, since I didn't treat the "problem" discursively at all. There was only a very brief preface which rebelled at "turning francs into dollars," and said the first things beginners ought to say. The scheme of the volume was two-fold: to make a set of avowedly literal translations as grubby as fidelity seems to demand—transliterate French staples into English; and then to put a pulse under the English and "translate the translations" in the sense that I tried to project qualities, identities, skills, predilections, textures—my own, such as they were, and Rimbaud's, such as I imagined them to be.

EH What Dryden called the "paraphrase" rather than literal translation or imitation.

BB I don't know whether either of those words really applies. It was something more subjective than imitation and more visceral than paraphrase. Meanwhile, I considered it a providence when I could exactly render in English what was literally present in the French. I had no conceptual stance that would lead me to say: "Here I'm going to paraphrase"; or "Here is where I imitate."

EH The scheme of the book, as you say, called for the literal rendering first.

BB   Only to indicate how inadequate poetry in its literal state can be—
to make the point that poetry was not *information*, that the translator's
task had only begun when all the facts of syntax and substance had been
reliably extrapolated. The point was to isolate *something else*—something
absent or missing—by maximizing the vacuum where all had been suspended in the search for meanings and was now in danger of disappearing entirely from the transaction: the power of imagination. How do you
imagine or reimagine the process of a poem's embodiment, the poem not
as an informative entity, but as a complex—I believe Coleridge called it
esemplastic—of immediate excitements that stand for a live experience?

EH   But evidently, if this work, as you describe it, was your first, you
already had a kind of theoretical and didactic interest in the subject—or
the "problem"—of translation.

BB   No, I would say I stumbled on translation simply in the process of
trying to find something that was cognate with my experience of having
thought about a poet, read him word for word and word by word, and
found it hostile or hateful to paraphrase. Let us say I invoked a "pleasure
principle" rather than a homiletic one, that my approach was hedonistic
rather than Aristotelian, much as Coleridge's is when he says the "immediate aim of poetry is pleasure not truth." I would be quite as ready to
say that the *immediate* aim of translation is pleasure not truth. Eventually,
of course, immediate pleasure proves to be Platonic rather than erotic,
and leads to imaginable truth. The two are not necessarily antithetical.

EH   Well, there you have a principle! It's very hard to get working
translators to say what they really think translation is for, or about. In
the case of poets, it's almost always an attempt to render the pleasure, the
experience of pleasure, *knowingly*. Were you aware at that time of any
sort of transfusion going on from your translations into your poems?

BB   Translation is a way of working and living, or writing and breath-
ing, and not a public benefaction. It would be altogether wishful to imagine I had turned into something Rimbaudian myself; but looking back at
my development at the time, I would say that there was a conspicuous
thrust—an infusion rather than a transformation—which was all to the
good. It may be all there to this day—but that is for others skilled in "the
anxieties of influence" to determine.

EH   Where do you fit it into your own oeuvre as a poet?

BB   In a limbo I vaguely remember as one of marked disjunctions and escalations of style that had something to do with my previous collision with Hart Crane in 1936. I sensed something then, which has now been abundantly researched and certified: that there had also been a collision of Rimbaud with Crane, and I was dizzy with the hovering ambiguity. I was already en route to a kind of impasto, or density, of language—crisscrossed by all the short circuits and shifts of speed I coveted in both the French of Rimbaud and the latter-day Elizabethan of Crane. The last poem to go into my first collection, a poem called "The Enemy Joy" at some times, and "Tarry, Delight" at others, was a direct outcome of my translation.

EH Now if I'm not mistaken, your reputation as a translator is based mainly on your translations from the Spanish, rather than the French or Italian.

BB True. However, in my long apprenticeship to Wallace Fowlie I read Baudelaire for the first time, Mallarmé, Valéry, Corbière. . . .

EH All the significant "moderns."

BB What we were really doing was *dowsing*. Wherever I picked up a possibility of water or gold or whatever, I made a decided bend in that direction.

EH There's another aspect that ought to concern us: this conjunction of three minds—Fowlie himself, and two poets sharing a literary experience involving an exchange of literatures.

BB In return for Rimbaud, I read Fowlie some of Hart Crane, whom he found more difficult than Valéry.

EH I had a conversation a few days ago with Herb Mason, who did a remarkable job of the *Gilgamesh* epic and whose languages are not modern or romantic, generally, but Arabic, Persian. . . . Mason came to the story of the *Gilgamesh* epic, which is mainly about the loss of a friend, partly as a result of his own personal losses, and for several years afterwards he kept sharing the poem with others. After four years of this, he was ready to write what he calls his verse-narrative based on the *Gilgamesh* epic. I hadn't been aware, till speaking with Mason, of how such a conjunction induces a strong, if gradual, drive to tackle the work, especially in the early phases of one's interest in translation.

BB I imagine it would differ in relation to the media in which the originals exist. Certainly, for poetry, I would say translation is neither a solitary voice nor a collective voice. It is an attempt to express one's own exuberance or one's own sense of contact with things. I myself don't know how to separate my own voice from the initiating voices because the initiating voices furnish a continuing motive for my own. There are two voices, two presences. That has never really changed; translation for me still remains the sensuous approximation of an amateur—a histrionic projection of my visceral and intellectual fascinations—and, I would always want to add, my *pleasure*.

EH   The pleasure could also be that of sharing something with the absent author whom one is translating. You translated Neruda later, and a great deal.

BB   Abundantly, because the man himself was abundant. Because no one else was doing it abundantly at the time. Because Neruda was pleased with the renderings and the choices, and abundantly encouraged me to translate.

EH   That's a case in which one knows one's source; I mean the "originating poet." Is there a difference, though, between posthumous and nonposthumous translations?

BB   I believe I have had a variety of such experiences, all certified. I translated an anthological selection of Rafael Alberti for the University of California Press and have a kind of illustrated scroll covered with doves and Andalusian promises in the special calligraphy of the poet to show for it. I translated a good part of the *Cántico* by Jorge Guillén, and had the pleasure of reading with him jointly at Bennington. He was good enough to fill fly-leaves of my copy of *Cántico* with translations of his own—Wallace Stevens, Joyce, Eliot—instead of doves and calligraphy. That translation, by the way, was done with the "midwifery" of Norman Thomas di Giovanni, who was endlessly self-effacing and diligent as an intermediary between translators and the poet: a permutation we haven't talked about as yet. There, the English was discussed in considerable detail by both Guillén and di Giovanni; we all revised and re-revised, until there was a kind of despairing agreement, or its English equivalent, on the text that was to stand next to the Spanish. The same was true of di Giovanni's later project on Borges, for which I was also enlisted. In the case of Borges, we *slaved* at a very special genre of translation that Borges had in mind as par for his course. Of course, Borges knows *better* English-English than we do, and certainly in other ways than we do—down to its Anglo-Saxon marrow, which he especially coveted in exchange for the Latinate marrow of his language. In the case of Borges, there was a change in the matrices of the two languages, as though he were subjecting the weight and temper of a Spanish, which he regarded as jejune, to an Anglo-Saxon decantation. If Borges had had his way—and he generally did—all polysyllables would have been replaced by monosyllables, especially in the third and fourth revisions, to which he often pressed his absent collaborators. People concerned about the legitimacy of the literal might well be scandalized by his mania for dehispanization.

EH He was using you as writing hands. . . .

BB "Simplify me. Modify me. Make me stark. My language often embarrasses me. It's too youthful, too Latinate. I love Anglo-Saxon. I want the wiry, minimal sound. I want monosyllables. I want the power of Cynewulf, Beowulf, Bede. Make me macho and gaucho and skinny." That sort of thing.

EH Did the period of Borges and di Giovanni follow the Guillén period?

BB Yes, by a number of years. Guillén was the first venture involving a stable of translators and a steward. Then di Giovanni undertook a similar venture with Borges—and something very Borgesian happened. First, he was devoured by Borges and the cadre of translators he had enlisted to transmit the specifications of Borges. Then, as a result of his proximity to the Master and the indescribable rigors of modifying and leveling the rest of us (for which we all have reason to be grateful), di Giovanni took to practicing the art copiously himself, as Borges's other Other, and outdid us all.

EH A very odd development. I'd like to go back, though, to what we were talking about in connection with your further work—the experience, then, of getting to know Spanish.

BB Well, it's the poets who have a way of making translators out of other poets, and poetry that leads them from one language to another. In my own case, it was Lorca who led me into Spanish—a decade after I first accepted a translation of him for the *Nation*. Then, ten years later, during a postwar Guggenheim in 1946–47, while I was at the University of Virginia as loafing poet-in-residence, I took a Spanish course and began to learn the language academically. Then, long before I should have, some would say—before I had brought my literacy to the point where it was theoretically desirable to translate—I simply flung myself at Lorca. I reversed the recommended procedure: I learned Spanish syntax in the act of pursuing the sounds, the idiosyncrasies, and the poetry of Lorca.

EH Yet you had previously translated Rimbaud with a man who is a master of the subject.

BB I believe I have served under many masters in translating from the Spanish, too—José Montesinos and Luis Monguió of the University of California in Berkeley, Ángel del Río, Paco García Lorca of Columbia, among others, as well as the poets themselves—in my encounters with the *duende* of Castilian. But I was at first quite solitary with the Lorca— with Lorca and the whole of Mexico, which I visited year after year, long before I made it to Spain, in those winter recesses conveniently provided by Bennington, to get the whole ambience of the language. I combined every conceivable form of circulation and ventilation of the language and the literature, tunneled in every conceivable direction to accelerate my faculty for using the language.

EH I believe your translation of Lorca's *Poet in New York* is dated 1955 and has since appeared in eighteen printings.

BB There's a connection between my prentice years in Lorca and *The Poet in New York* which I should mention. Donald Allen, then of Grove Press, had read my translations in *Quarterly Review of Literature* and was the first to approach me with the idea of translating the whole of the *Poeta* for Grove. It seemed to me an extravagant compliment and an utterly reckless undertaking for everyone concerned. In the end I said, "Why not?" I was enlisted to translate *Poet in New York* by a man who had the wit and the uncanny facility of sensing what are generally called "vogues" or waves in the making, and later turn out to be total landslides of taste—like his later anthology of the "poets since 1945" and the canonization of Ginsberg.

EH If I recall correctly, Rolfe Humphries's translation was also bilingual and preceded the first edition of Bergamín in Mexico.

BB By a nose, I believe: both should be postmarked about 1940. The long story of the search for a canon for *Poet in New York* and its relation to the scenario provided by Humphries in his persevering and indispensable edition is enormously complicated. There is a detailed chronology of it in my own edition for Grove, and the transaction is again being reexamined by a cadre of French and Spanish hispanists in Madrid, whose job it is to invent an authorized text for all Lorca. At the same time, it has been turned into a tour de force of detection by Daniel Eisenberg, a young scholar working against the international grain from Florida State University. I soon saw that the job of piecing together the potsherds in Mexico and the United States for a provisional text was also inseparable from the ordeal of translating it. A number of poems still remain fixed in the canon, either by fiat from Madrid, or by the labor of maverick scholars. To the very last moment of publication, "New York poems," lost, purloined, apocryphal, or hoarded by their possessive and unpredictable custodians, continued to show up in odd places like Mallorca. I especially remember a sophisticated bookstore on Calle Madero in Mexico City where I routinely asked for South American books about Lorca, and was told: "We have some copies of the original Mexican edition of *Poeta en Nueva York* on hand." Just imagine! Stored away in that bookstore there must have been some thirty or forty copies of the Editorial Seneca edition of the *Poeta*—retired, rather than remaindered, because of vanished Mexican interest and the apathy of everyone concerned! They were glad to give me a dozen for the equivalent of about eighty cents apiece—all of which I have since given away to deserving connoisseurs: all but one. Such are the adventures of canon makers who turn up at the right time and get lucky!

EH As before, when we were talking about translations of Rimbaud and you mentioned Hart Crane, another bell struck, because I'd always thought of Hart Crane as the nodal center in the development of modern poetry, someone very significant, especially for the people starting to write in that period. That is, Crane stands with Pound and Eliot as one of the chief transmitters of European traditions, however imperfectly.

BB However, we all know now that Crane was semiliterate in those languages himself and lacked the sophistication of mentors like Allen Tate and Yvor Winters, who could have taken him to sources, as Wallace Fowlie took me. There was that linguistic and intuitional seepage, though, that bloodletting, and that was enough for Crane. I mean his capacity to devour, his gusto, his faith in the pleasure principle: all operated like Braille, as a tactile accelerator of good things.

EH Yes. When I spoke to Robert Lowell some years ago, he said that Hart Crane was the first American poet who meant something to him.

BB I would say the same.

EH I had that experience, too. But with Lorca, we have to do with the happenstance of a Spanish poet writing a totally aberrant work about New York, a city that he happened to occupy with Crane in 1929. A strange situation—a European infusion concentrating on urban life in a way that rediscovered New York to the New Yorkers and surrealism for a displaced Andalusian.

BB Like New York's gift of Washington Irving to the Alhambra and the Caliphate of Granada.

EH Don't you think Lorca's surrealism is the definitive development of his late phase—both the *Poet in New York*, and those last and "lost" plays?

BB Certainly it is the timely antidote for that provincial Andalusian *gitanismo* that enchanted Lorquistas all over the world and drove Lorca himself to surrealist despair. The episode is traumatic, if not definitive. But I think it is also related to other trends on the way out because, perhaps, of new tastes pressing toward the center from the periphery, searching for hot spots: people like Crane.

EH Yes. Also the whole phenomenon has changed with regard to Latin America. You, for example, went ahead to Pablo Neruda after Lorca—a continuity totally understandable in terms of subsequent developments. What I'm trying to get at is that you, in your experience, career, and craft as a poet and translator, have not only incorporated poets in Spanish, but also started something of a trend—even after my own translations and my New Directions book on Lorca came out in 1944.

BB I often flinch at the consequences. Not long ago, I heard from a graduate student in English at the University of California at Berkeley who thought Ginsberg and the San Francisco sound were the summit of all American modernity. He was perfectly certain in his own mind that my translation of *Poet in New York* was the swinger that set Ginsberg off and then lit up the whole western seaboard like a switchboard. I wrote him back denying it as icily as I could, hoping it was not so. I haven't heard from him since. He was utterly wishful and tendentious about the whole thing. He found, for example, that the publication dates of *Howl* and *Poet in New York* were almost simultaneous: "Couldn't Ginsberg have read your translations in magazine form?" he wanted to know. Well, he could have—in *Poetry*, the *Virginia Quarterly Review*, *Partisan Review*: but I was firm and said I didn't think that's what touched off "poetry since '45."

EH Well, there's some strange alchemical transmutation when a "new poetry" arrives at the right time or someone picks up the poet who can transform the whole movement of things. I think we both may have had something to do with the infusion of Spanish into English for American and English poetry, via Lorca: a development vital to the internationalization of poetry.

BB Certainly Neruda believed I was rendering him a cosmopolitan service, and gave me carte blanche in the choice and execution of volume after volume, except in the one case when he urged me to share a book with Alastair Reid to blend American translation with British. He even insisted that I was the only one to translate his first and only play into the kind of theater and poetry he intended, while I spent two years debating the same premise myself. The fact that I undertook the translation of *Joaquín Murieta* can hardly be called a phase in the development of international poetry, however! That was a very personal failure.

EH But Neruda saw that you were not only doing him a service. You were providing a bridge to North American poetry, as Crane might have wished it to be.

BB Once, Ted Roethke startled me by asking Howard Nemerov to "Tell Belitt that his *Poet in New York* is a kind of Bible to my kids [at the University of Washington]." Was that another phase of the San Francisco backlash, or the solid hegemony of cosmopolitan taste?

EH There have recently appeared other translators of Neruda: a small cadre of them, one might say.

BB That's all to the good. It's what I'd hoped for—many sounds, many orientations and intonations, many biases (rather than vendettas), many permutations of pleasure—a whole orchestra tuning up on processes and procedures. But recent translations have all been on the side of a puristic leveling of Neruda to the letter of the literal word. Neruda is sacrosanct to his American idolators.

EH You mean Tarn, Bly, Walsh. . . .

BB Translators, as I have somewhere observed, are an anthropophagous species who know how to devour their own kind. But I think the choral rendering of Neruda is encouraging because tolerance and abundance are fixed points and terminal goals of translation.

EH When you went to Neruda, did you have to wrench your style—

did you have to think of a way of doing it that was different from the way you'd done other poems?

BB I never know how translation ought to be done before I have begun to do it; though the "wrench" was immediately apparent to me. The posture of translation has to be inductive, I think. If the sound is right and carries with it my whole engrossment as a poet, translation has a way of falling into place, in the same way that poems do. I have no program unless it is one of leading naively and obsessively with the whole stock of my resources as a poet writing poetry. How else can one survive the punishing trajectory of a whole book that selects the best of four or five volumes at a time for anthological display and delectation—a jolting set of texts, some of which are right for you, others of which are tedious, or with tedious stretches? As a translator in bulk, one must move with equal plausibility through hot and cold, through what is congenial and what's remote, roll with the punches on some least common denominator of continuing energy. One *can't* be Nobody in Particular. I see no other way to do it.

EH You're temperamentally more akin to the lyric poems.

BB Well, politics was never my motive for translating Neruda; and surrealism is not my dish of tea.

EH Those endless pileups of metaphors!

BB Metaphors excite me in any form; and there's a special magic in the divination of surrealist metaphors, which are really a kind of irrational metaphysics or therapeutic shorthand: like reading entrails or tea leaves. In the case of *Poet in New York* I found some sections overstated, too facilely or too hysterically surrealist—until I began to read the poem as an irreversible autobiography of alienation, by a poet who exquisitely embodied one culture and was made to collide with its antithesis here. It is a psychological document, an ethnical *pesadilla* whose real passion and significance as an idiom lies in its queasy transcription of horror and loss and panic, without the mediation of prudence.

EH It's a remarkable poem, and still, perhaps, will never be wholly assimilated; a little like "Song of Myself" (which gets a lot of currency nowadays at universities in a way it never did twenty or thirty years ago)—a poem that is probably about the same length as *Poeta en Nueva York*. Structurally, say—all fifty-two sections of Whitman can be accounted for. I wonder if that will ever happen to the *Poeta*.

BB   Let us say that it is the fate of the vanguard to move to the center; and universities are a vehicle of that movement. At first reading, one feels such poems are always *ahead* of one—that is part of their exasperating attraction: something to be sniffed out, or be shaken by: then a "classic" moves out from under, to become the signature of one's "modernity."

EH   But speaking of "psychological documents" and collision courses between Lorca and other cultures barbarous or exotic to him, I wonder what *is* the text actually translated? Put it another way: is the text always a stable quantity, or is it that, plus something else—a variable? And if one says that it's also a variable quantity, then does one have to adjust, as a translator, not only to a word-for-word persistence of the text, but also to its ups and downs, its hiatuses and gravitational shifts? There are two observations to be made here: first, that something else begins to emerge before the final translation comes into being: the translator's own psychological relationship to the text; and second, the fact that you can't expect faithfulness where there's not something to be faithful to: some redoubtable scenario. Not even the mind of God can be thought of as the single originating source. According to the Cabala, God is Absence.

BB   Or floating somewhere in the middle of the air in a visionary bath, or on a divan of enigmas. It's the Platonism, the Idea of the Perfect Poem, or the Perfect Word, that I think interferes with the sweaty labor of translation, the sweaty empiricism in which everything is an action, a commitment, a deed, a choice, and refuses to exist abstractly in the realm of the Potential. One translates as Forster's Professor Godbole prays, singing one's odd little tune and saying: "Come! Come! Come! Come!" One has to intrude upon possibility; even the poem speaks in its own right, at its most expressive pitch, as a pure tissue of possibility. The translator provides the possibles, probables, utterances, and then tries to anchor the whole floating realm of epistemological possibility. I insist it's an epistemological, rather than a semantic or linguistic: What kind of knowledge does poetry involve? What is the *thing* that translators can know, and how can their language know it? What is the syntax for its survival as either immediate pleasure or eventual truth? The knowledge must never be falsified: it is a confidence, a trust—but there is a human need to take a stand and mediate knowledge. All translation, at its best, is mediation rather than definition.

EH Then we're back to that question of whether the interpreter is. . . .

BB Well, I wasn't thinking in terms of exegetical interpretation alone. In the realm of epistemological discourse, poems exist in order to invite and release inexhaustible probability. Translation should operate with similar exposure to probability. Putting a pulse under your language like tubing for a blood transfusion, working rhythmically and feelingly for the formalization of the forces that give the intentionality of language and sound to the probable—the whole sonic bit—is part of that "knowledge." To what degree can such things be known? How does one consolidate the sonic integrity of a thing in the act of translating it? There's the fascination of translation. On the other hand, one can hardly argue that because a thing is provisional, one has a license, poetic or otherwise, to multiply chaos. But where provisionality abounds (I sound like Saint Paul talking about grace!), the determinations have to remain suspended or vague. One is merely faith-full: as faithful as one can be under circumstances that don't moralize as much as, say, dogma does. The operative word is *faith*, and not *fidelity*.

EH You're saying something very interesting to me in connection with the desire of the original poet to express something that, as we all know, never got expressed; or possibly exceeded the poet. When a poet sees a translation of his work, his interest in the poem as a work-in-progress momentarily rekindles. He says to his translator: You go ahead and maybe you'll find . . . perhaps what I left out, or what leaped ahead of me. That, I suppose, is another touch of comedy that makes all utterance kin.

BB Something very similar happens to me when a Nerudist or a Lorquist gives me the exegesis of the poem as a track to ride a translation on, or a thread through the maze of impersonated fidelities. I myself remain curious about the thing *I myself* am contriving. I don't know where my labors will take me, and I certainly don't know how the original ought to have been *translated*, before or after the fact. I take my lumps as a translator, hoping as I go that nothing has really been violated and that the proportions of the original have been maintained even though my own dynamics have merged with the poet's. I wear my conscience where it belongs: at the tip of my pen, and not on my sleeve like a medieval garter.

EH How would you test whether a work of translation is faithful or has a right to exist in its own terms, whatever its relation to the original work? Is there any test?

BB What is the test for the *Rubáiyát of Omar Khayyám*? There is nothing as blue and red as litmus paper. There are signs, faits accomplis, reassurances: for one thing, volatility; responsibility, for another, the certainty that all the elements have been subjected to atomic scrutiny—all the words as they pass from their moorings in the Spanish into the ink of the translation, with no leaps of convenience or deletions such as you might find in the *Imitations* of Lowell.

EH He's taken that word from Dryden, and Dryden means an "adaptation."

BB I've written as curiously as I could on that subject, to explore my own criteria of translation. I've weighed the forfeits of expressive translation as against the privations of anonymous translation: "translation as a personal mode," against "the translator as nobody in particular." *Both* are ploys, impersonations, heuristic deceptions.

EH Can you go into that further?

BB I would let the pieces speak for themselves as I wrote them,[11] rather than paraphrase off the top of my head. In the case of Lowell's *Imitations* I wanted to consider the kind of option that deliberately subordinates the translated poet to the identity of the translator and in which the intent is, as it were, binaural: to provide two voices for one. Lowell has opted even more flamboyantly for *one* continuous voice, indelibly and conspicuously his own, when he is translating as he pleases from the whole canon of European and Mediterranean masterpieces.

EH Then later he amalgamates his translations into the body of his own poetry.

BB I see it as a kind of dramatism—a histrionic or supportive use of "the individual talent" of the original at a time when, for one reason or another, the translator's initiative has lapsed or sagged or withdrawn from easy accessibility to lick its wounds. What follows, I think, is an expedient—a desperate—use of translation to compensate for the translator's blockages: to keep a big talent moving and perform all the feats that have to do with the whole repertory of poetry, rather than the special register of his own oeuvre. "Translation as trampoline"—or, as I suggested in the beginning, a "jungle gym."

EH I have two feelings about that, myself: one of them is that Lowell was wrong to do it, because he gave translation a bad reputation at a time when it needed more imaginative support. But also, that he was right to do it because he went way out on a limb and thereby anticipated a center for corrective discussion and work on the part of other translators at a time when the issues were confused.

BB I think that large talents have less choice in such matters than the middling or unharried ones. Lowell's motive was self-preservation, survival rather than charity. I value that enormously.

EH But as a practice for others, it has its good and bad sides.

BB It does. What I try to suggest in my article is that much of what Lowell did was, basically, *translation* in the old-fashioned sense, despite the strange aberrations and gerrymanders that result from jettisoning what was incompatible. In Lowell's case, I yield to the urgency that leads major talents to prey on the identities and styles of other great talents, as an armature for their own utterance. Only think of the many disguises of Blake and Keats for preying on Milton, and Neruda for preying on Whitman!

EH I suppose Lowell was doing in his own way what Pope and Dryden were doing with Homer and Vergil in their own time. Pumping their own poetic juices—not to mention their prosody!—into the text.

BB I think in many ways Lowell is more faithful than Pope or Dryden.

EH All one can hope to develop is some sense of the immediate goals that are involved *in* translation and *for* translation, quite apart from matters of public benefits or eventual public worth. The fallacy of translation as something that is "deceptive" and a "betrayal" of an original—we all know the Italian for it—can really be understood as part of a creative undertaking—creative, not in the wild sense, though sometimes that is important, too, but as the transfiguring of invention. That seems to have kept *you* working for years!

BB There must be some allowable ambience of *pluralism* in the whole premise of multicultural translation.

EH Yes.

BB Personally, I work out of the premise that there is no universal motive, like "fidelity," which all translation should serve, stopping its ears to the siren song of diversity and oddity. We serve a multiple, and not a univocal, function. . . . We translate to accomplish different ends.

For the functions do differ. Some translate in order to exist supinely on the opposite side of the page as a trot to pace subservient readers who cannot or will not construe the language and meanings for themselves, or check back with a dictionary and a grammar. Others translate to deepen their own progressive absorptions in a sustaining talent: there is a vast body of translation in which the enlightened disclosure of admiration is primary—a kind of substantive embodiment of *praise*. Certainly, the eminent and odd, like Rilke, Pope, Baudelaire, Lowell, have always been allowed their own keyboard and predominant sound.

EH   Yes.

BB   But poets who are less than monumental themselves are interlopers!

EH   It's a question of bravura. The actor interlopes on the play and the people admire the performance because they have come to see the performance, and not because they are calculating "fidelity to Shakespeare" at every stage of the play. There are live translators and dead ones, and there are established world classics, or scenarios, to which they both turn, which interest us all. We all know that translations decay as styles decay.

BB   That's a crucial consideration, I think. One must always translate *inside* the wide-open premise that *re*-translation is always going on. If one realized the poignancy and the perishability of all translation, the built-in obsolescence of the search for contemporaneity, the premise of unalterable models like a Newtonian universe or the equation for energy would be scrapped. We would realize that the vocation of translators is a *comic* one. Comic in the sense that they are in an absurd situation in which they begin pietistically with the demure proviso that is part of every translator's apology for the translation: "I'm engaged in what I know is an impossible transaction. Of course, my original was innate to the identity of its creator and the language which embodied it. It is epistemologically and imaginatively irreducible, unrepeatable. It can't be translated." Then one immediately sets about translating it, as if all were really possible: *that's* comic! The critic then adds to the comedy by insisting in advance of the fact that Neruda, let us say, or Lorca, must be present in his own person, and cannot be simulated; or that his Spanish can never be functionally or prosodically secondary to the translator's English, just as Spanish cannot be derivative of English. And somewhere apart from it all sits the Sphinx of Translation herself, compounding the enigma with a final riddle which dooms positivists and optimists equally: "You have forfeited the language of the original from the very start. You cannot therefore expect to recover the original talent. What walks on four legs in the morning, on two in the noon, and on three in the total darkness of midnight, is Translation."

EH   What would you say to the metaphor of a pianist playing Chopin, as another permutation?

BB   What would you say to Rimski-Korsakov's orchestration of a theme by Moussorgsky?

EH   We may have all been too exclusive, puristic, blind, in our view of what originality always and only is. That may be at the source of our prejudice not only against certain translators and their work, but against the whole notion of translation as a "discipline." As you say, there's a certain daring and absurdity translators invite which others find—

BB   That dilemma of absurdity! All translators knowingly participate in it, all openly confess it: it is one of the hazards of the occupation. Yet still the purists bear down on the translator as though translation had no right to be what Neruda expressly claimed for his own poetry: *impure*, fallible. And still the translator plaintively explains, "But I am only trying to bring back Neruda and survive!"

EH   It's a strange duplicity that works against the person who's trying to rescue something called pleasure and ally it to meaning and genius. What the critic does is say: "This man is doing a very bad job of rendering something which I know exists in the original in a different way. *Traditore!*" But the critic is able to say that only because the translator has accepted the comedy, as you put it, with the seriousness of all good comedians, and has made possible something that would never have existed if the translator had adopted the obvious and meaningless premise: "This can't be accepted as the original."

BB   That way, the whole phenomenon of translation would lose its way for all time in the wilderness of "duplicity." That way, all language would lead us back to bedlam or babel again. No. There must be a workable dissemination of the world's avowedly irrecoverable originals. There must be a responsible tolerance and curiosity—a *skepticism*—regarding the ways in which all translation may happen, in the search for a shared humanity.

EH Your word *pluralism* can stand as a motto for what is needed. Not only a variety of translators and styles, but a sense that, whatever the relationship is, it must take place with more figures than a one-to-one equivalence.

BB It is very enlightening for translators to *be* translated in kind—like the therapy of psychoanalysis is first made to rebound on the potential psychiatrist, in his pursuit of the analysand. I often wish that on all literalists. There's nothing more depressing than an over-awed literalist at work on your own poetry. Whenever my verse is translated by others, I leave a long, loose rein, and urge translators to follow some powerful lead of their own: to put their poems together from beginning to end and calculate the thrusts in their own momentum, to find a brio that guarantees a continuum *for them* as well as for me. At times I have been led to approximate or revise myself in the Spanish of some inadequate translation—to make up in Spanish something I did not write originally, as the only way out of my English. Having tried on that shoe, I'm more convinced than ever of my jittery stock of "premises." No one is more tolerant of a translation, I've found, than the poet translated. He is the first to disbelieve in the whole venture, and marvel at the salvage. "*Of course* you can't do what I do, as I have done it! How perfectly extraordinary that you get anything accomplished at all! Just give me a little character, for heaven's sake! Just bring me back alive! Make readers pay attention and follow through. Be imaginative. Write as well as you can." *He* gets the comedy! Imagination isn't a phenomenon that can be limited to the poem in its original state. As a translator, it is legitimate, it is imperative, to work imaginatively, joyfully, energetically, ingeniously, patiently, inventively, yourself. Imagination cannot be present in the original only, and absent from the equivalence.

EH And of course, imagination is the most—

BB —risky and most daring, the most desired and mistrusted faculty: the most dangerous. We mistrust it but we can't renounce it. How can we afford to renounce imagination in the midst of a process we know to be absurd and inimitable? Or avoid saying to ourselves, in the awful solitude of translation, with an upbeat of nausea and wonder: "Well, I don't know for a *fact* what the poet knew, but I believe I can *imagine* how this might sound in my language." That's an honest and poignant transaction.

EH   John Hollander said that the theory of translation must involve a theory of literature; that when you talk about translation you have to assume there are readers willing to play the game.

BB   Exactly so. Who would deny a poet the risks and the pleasures of the imagination at every stage of the process that produced the poem? How can a translator assume that the poet has "done all that for me" in advance of the translation, and then block up his passage through other minds and languages? Only in imagination—here's Keats again!—does the translator wake up, like the poet, and find all is "true," as in Adam's dream.

EH   Have you ever written a poem based on a poem in Spanish but which, say, you don't have at hand and which you're not at the moment thinking of as a translation?

BB   Now that's a very curious question! There are translations "after" the poets they invoke—long after! At other times I am paid the lethal compliment of being found "better than the original," whatever that is. I wince at that; but I understand how such delusions arise, out of the translator's need to explain and complete meanings, as well as report them—meanings that need never be *chosen* in the original language precisely because they have accommodated themselves to that language.

EH   Isn't it a large-mindedness we hope for from the reader?

BB   It's curiosity I ask for—basic curiosity: what Kierkegaard called the "infinite interest in realities not one's own." In so far as the text itself has been touched by the imagination, it can never be definitive—that is another part of the comedy and another part of the forest. Meanings will always be viewed at different angles and in different ways by different critics, different centuries, different encounters. There is no single, originating, authentic locus of all the meanings. A poem is an *area*, a quantum, rather than a datum. It's an artifact, too—yes—but the artifact is what one can never wholly repossess: it remains unique to the language and the mind that put it together, and keeps aloof. Everything else is apocryphal. I'm perfectly willing to live with that, and dowse my way through a world of equivalences. Translation forces ambiguity upon one. It is up to the translator to enjoy the *nausée* of ambiguity and use it in objective and visceral ways to assemble an ambiguous circumstance: the coexistence of two improvising identities touching each other in equal but alien ways for purposes of imagination and pleasure. One

can never hope for terminal completions. Nothing has been terminated.
All is yet to come: all readers and critics are already at work construing
the experience differently. No one concludes a translation, any more
than one does the original.

EH   Well, that's a principle I find very useful, helpful, and resolving.

BB   However, translators have to *live*; they have to stay alive while
handling the disintegrating energy of identities other and more powerful
than their own, or be demolished by them. If they can match their innate
and inevitable self with something that is other than themselves, they
may be able to get on with a complex work. I'm not talking about the oc-
casional translator who can afford to be categorical because all he will
ever take on are isolated pieces, rather than whole books. What is dis-
maying is the volume confronted from beginning to end: "You mean to
say I have to translate *everything*?" "Yes, everything."

EH   "Eat every drop on your plate!" Who's to say that?

BB   I must say that to myself—and move through all of it, every bit of
it, with the same appearance of consanguinity.

EH   Exactly. You make a very strong case for what you actually do as
a translator, and that's exactly what I was hoping for in talking to you.

BB   But one thing I'm convinced of, after having written a great number
of prefaces, none of which has been read by reviewers or critics: translation is a provisional art. All my premises are provisional. I ask to be
judged in terms of what I initially set out to do and what I initially con-
cede you cannot expect of me.

EH   And it's interesting to consider how the translator's own premises
can change. There are three figures to be mentioned in this respect—
Nabokov, Borges, and Beckett. Nabokov and Beckett are probably
closer to each other than to Borges—but in the sense of multilingual
writers, those three are continually confronting their work in terms of
what *else* it might be, and, in fact, what else it has to become when, say,
Beckett translates himself into English or French.

BB   Yes, that's interesting. They sit in the doorway of Janus, or
Tiresias. How does a translator behave when translating *himself* from one
"original" to another?

EH   He does what any other translator would do, I suspect, even if he
were not translating his own work. It's generally considered a bad idea—

to translate your own work. Maybe that is the doorway of Narcissus. What he does is to re-create it.

BB And is often faithless to the original!

EH There was someone who hit Robert Lowell over the head—I think it was Guy Daniels[12]—for having deliberately misread in his translation of it a poem of Anna Akhmatova. It infuriated her, according to Daniels—not because of any personal injury, but because Lowell violated something she was trying to say in the poem that had a specific humanistic relevance in her experience.

BB Well, we've already ruled out quixotic or capricious substitutions. We've agreed that the poet has a right to protest to his translator (Lord knows about *imitators*!): "You've been close to me all the way so far. You *owe* me. . . ."

EH ". . . the rules of the game, the ground base." But in line with what you were saying before about Borges—his desire to recast his work by surrogate means, deliberately—

BB I think it was quite proper for Borges to carry his translators into the labyrinth with him, as a comedian rather than a tragedian, and pursue his known curiosity regarding all fictive outcomes—especially "the supreme fiction." His comic stance, regarding both the language of his youth and our somber translations of it, had the right ring of sobering facetiousness. He meant it seriously. It is the function of comedy to dwell upon vices, affectations, foibles.

EH Of course, he wrote the central fable about translation in "Pierre Menard"; so he's a very important sibyl in this whole bilingual mystery.

BB Borges was always the first to question: *Who* is the author of *what*— and for how long? In the same way, it is serious and fruitful to ask: Was Borges the author of di Giovanni—because by some magic known to them both he invaded the identity of di Giovanni and translated them both into Siamese?

EH Again, it's something "histrionic," as you say: a dramatistic use of personae.

BB And a philosophical one. In so far as Borges himself was aware of his equivocations—of originating and repudiating Borges, and then translating him by proxy—he forced the question precisely to the point where it ought to exist for all translators. Mimesis is only one permutation of translation in the long and impossible itinerary of Languages in Search of an Author. Let's grant the play is Pirandello's; but the fiction is Borges's own, just as the double of an apocryphal Juan de Mairena was Machado's. . . . It is Borges who makes the real point and haunts us forever after—that language in itself is provisional; only Borges, who has seen the emperor naked under his verbal clothing. It's Borges who tells us the translator has a responsibility to provisionality—that he must draw needle and thread through an invisible cloth, work without a false sense of having somehow *circumvented* the provisional in the act of translation, of having completed the poet in a way that the poet himself did not. It's the critics who are interested in completion and the literal, and poets who say: "Adieux! The fancy cannot cheat so well / As she is famed to do. . . ." In this sense the translation of poetry can never exceed the enigma of it, and be true.

EH   The play's the thing: the interplay.

BB   From *ludere*: to play; or *interludium*: the play in between the play. All translation is ludic, and not ethical. It turns into play the moment one moves out of the language of the original—the most serious play imaginable, since all knowledge hangs in the balance, or waits in the wings: the play with language, and possibility with utterance.

EH   Very good.

BB   Why not leave it at that? Much good will come of it, as Howard Nemerov, who once called translation a "desperate system of double-entry bookkeeping," or something close to that, likes to say enigmatically.

EH   The good of unused distance? Of detachment?

BB   The good of playing the game like a true gambler, for risk and pleasure. The good of chastening misgiving.

EH   Well, perhaps the best place to conclude a conversation about poetry and translation is with a novel of Melville's—who was no slouch at enigmas himself. *The Confidence Man*, which I've always thought his best work, ends, I believe: "Something more will come of this masquerade."

BB   That's the tone. Confidence is the name of the game.

Clemens Kalischer

5 / Richard Wilbur

EH   I was reading the introduction to your translations of *The Misanthrope* and *Tartuffe*, and I noticed you said about the necessity of using the couplet that *The Misanthrope* required it because the work is so epigrammatic, while *Tartuffe* is less so.

RW   Yes. I think there are fewer moments of deliberate wit in *Tartuffe*, and so the requirement that one keep rhyme and meter for the sake of epigrammatic snap is a little less. Still, there's a good deal of that quality in anything that Molière wrote, so I wouldn't think of putting any of his verse plays into prose.

EH   Even though he was not a poet outside of the plays?

RW   Very little, I think. He did (I believe) write a number of lyrics and some little verses, but no, he wasn't really a poet outside of the plays, and inside the poetic plays he's a very prosaic poet in many respects. I guess I said in one of the introductions that, by contrast to someone like Racine, he's almost free of figurative language: he also doesn't use key words, thematic words, in the vigorous way that Racine does, although some mistaken critic, I suppose, might want to argue about that with me. In any case, it makes Molière much easier to translate than Racine would be, not merely because he's comedy (and somehow rhyme consorts more readily with comedy than tragedy) but also because you don't have to wrestle with difficult figures and key words quite so much.

EH   There are many interesting things about those translations that I would like to come back to a little later. Meanwhile, may I ask what your original contact with the idea of translation was? That is, how you conceived of it when you started. Not necessarily with Molière, but earlier. I know you did other things earlier.

RW I think my first experience with translation was when André du Bouchet, who's now a rather well-established French poet, and I, were fellow graduate students at Harvard. I had picked up enough French from basic courses, and reading, and being in France during World War II, so that I felt able to make a start on most French poems. So I would sit around with André, trying to translate his poems into English, and he sat around trying to translate mine into French. And it was a nice way to begin one's career as a translator. Not that I did anything that was any good, but knowing André I was able to begin the translation of any one of his poems with a sense that I knew his tones of voice and his preoccupations.

EH What you say immediately strikes a chord because now, almost every time I've spoken with a poet who's translated, there has been an experience of working with someone at the beginning, whether a friend or an inciting informant. In the case of Ben Belitt, who began with Wallace Fowlie, the challenge was to please his informant who was interested in the early modern poets—Rimbaud particularly—who hadn't been translated very well. So that the relationship was the immediate instigation not only to do the translations but also to do them very well.

RW I suppose that, Fowlie being a translator of the French himself, they must have been vying a little bit. They were having a *concours*, weren't they?

EH Well, I don't know what the circumstances were. I had the impression that Fowlie wanted verse translations that stood up on their own. Whether he had done Rimbaud in verse or prose, I don't know. Later on Belitt worked on other poets, but in this connection he got to know some of them personally. This was the stimulus for him to do Neruda, for example.

RW He got to know Neruda personally? Yes, I think that's terribly important. I couldn't imagine beginning to translate anybody living or dead without at least having the illusion of some kind of personal understanding—some understanding of the range of his feelings beyond the particular work. That's hard, of course, in the case of someone like du Bellay, one of whose poems I recently translated. But even in his case

I did develop an adequate sense of background and of the emotional set in which the poem was made.

EH   Does that mean that you almost always translate from poets you have a sense of identity with?

RW   Yes, I think so. I suspect I have to like the poem pretty well in the first place. This keeps me, I think, from being a professional translator—doing things wholesale. I have to like the poem and feel it has something to do with my feelings—that I understand the feelings that went into it. Perhaps, also, I like it and am particularly well motivated when I feel the poem represents, as it were, an extension or stretching of my own emotional possibilities.

EH   You emphasize something that Belitt also suggested as a prime motivation for doing the poem—pleasure, pleasure in doing it, rather than gain, but gain as it might happen through pleasure.

RW   Monetary gain is always unexpected, I suppose, in the translation business, though I imagine it's better paid now than it used to be, isn't it?

EH   I don't know.

RW   But you don't think of pay . . . at any rate, someone like me who translates individual poems by different people out of various languages is obviously not proceeding in a businesslike manner. I'm just responding to things that catch my eye or have been brought to my attention. Sometimes people who have a feeling for what I'm like, or what my work is like, are fairly accurate about prescribing what I should attempt. For example, Simon Karlinsky wrote me a while back about doing a number of poems by the exiled Russian poet Nikolai Morshen, since he saw some affinities too; Karlinsky is a very good finger man. I found Max Hayward to be similarly gifted in matching the translator to the poem. The Voznesensky poems that he and Patricia Blake once picked out for me to do were pretty much the right ones.

EH   I see. Well, that goes along with other incidents of the same kind I know about. I want to go back now to your beginnings as a translator. Your first experience translating had to do with the poems of a friend, the French poet du Bouchet. Then, after that, what happened?

RW   I think my early efforts at translation had largely to do with the French, because that was the only foreign language of which I possessed anything; though of that I had a very faulty knowledge, and still do.

EH It was school French?

RW School French fortified by the French a soldier picks up during war experience. I remember translating some little poems of Villiers de l'Isle-Adam, an author to whom du Bouchet had directed my attention. I had an anthology of great old chestnuts of the French tradition, and found in it an ode of La Fontaine's that appealed to me a good deal and. . . .

EH You just picked these out, as you were looking through.

RW . . . just picked them out. As they say—they grabbed me. Having done La Fontaine's "Ode to Pleasure," I asked Harry Levin to see if I'd gotten the words right. He kindly helped me as he had helped Marianne Moore . . . or perhaps was to help; I forget at what time he began to help her with her French translations. He was always generous with that kind of aid. I tried to do a little Catullus around 1949 or so, but I had no luck with it. I can't stand the mincing and evasive translations of his tougher poems that one has in the Loeb Library; at the same time I couldn't find a way to be nasty in a language that was poetically effective.

EH Why did you want to translate Catullus?

RW I'd always been fascinated by particular tones of his. He does not seem to me to be a terribly broad sensibility, but a great deal of personality transpires from his poetry as it does, say, from Villon—another example of a person who is not very broad but is very strong.

EH Then the kind of interest you developed in translation came from similar desultory lookings into books and advice from people who wrote you or asked you to do it.

RW Well, the askings came later after I'd done a certain number of poems, more or less by accident. That is, through falling in love with them myself or through having someone say, "Have a look at this." I suppose I began to be invited to do poems in translation after I had done *The Misanthrope* translation, which was published in 1955. People began to think of me as an available translator—someone who, with a little linguistic aid, might do things out of languages he didn't know.

EH So that was the first significant translation you did.

RW Yes. There are translations sprinkled through my second book, *Ceremony*, and my third book, *Things of This World*. But there aren't too many of them, really. I suppose I began to be thought of as a laborer in that vineyard when *The Misanthrope* came out. . . . I must qualify that.

I do remember now that when I was living out in the town of Corrales, New Mexico, which we both know so well, Jackson Mathews wrote me and said he was putting together for New Directions a collection of *The Flowers of Evil* of Baudelaire, and that he wasn't quite satisfied with the existing versions of the great chestnut poems, the "Invitation to the Voyage," "Correspondences," and "The Albatross." He asked me to try them. So I tried them. That was 1952.

EH Did you feel that you had *done* the job—that is, was he satisfied with them?

RW He was satisfied with them, though I remember Jack saying that my reaching for a rhyme in the "Correspondances" poem had obliged me to refer to a "child's caress" in a way that would have offended Baudelaire's fastidiousness. But he liked them all right and used them in that anthology. And I was satisfied with "L'Invitation au voyage." Though I thought, "Of course, it's a failure," I thought that it was a less ludicrous failure than the attempts of others.

EH Yes, one has to measure one's success by the failures of others, even of one's own. One of the things that interests me in the translation of poetry is the way a very scrupulous translator who has a strong poetic voice of his own (and I think you fit this description) cannot escape merging his voice with that of the poet he is translating. What do you feel? Do you deliberately try to suppress your own style in translating?

RW I think that I do try to avoid putting into anyone else's poem, as I bring it across into English, mannerisms of my own, and I certainly try to efface myself as much as possible. I shouldn't like to seem to be demonstrating that Voznesensky could write like Wilbur if he'd only try. What I say to myself—not too dishonestly, I hope—is that I'm putting whatever abilities I have at the service of the poem I'm translating, and that because I feel some kind of affinity with him, or at least with the particular work I'm rendering, that I *can* use such words as readily come to me without imposing myself on the work. I can give an example of this. I can contrast myself with Ezra Pound in this respect. Ezra Pound translated Voltaire's poem to Madame du Châtelet, turning it into a kind of imagistic prose poem. Some of the effects are quite brilliant and charming. He takes everything that is abstract and makes it concrete. When there's a reference to love, for example, capitalized Love (and Voltaire is really thinking of statues of Eros in a garden), Pound puts lovers on the grass.

EH Where they belong.

RW Yes. I translated the same poem, trying—without using antique language, without sounding eighteenth-century—to transmit it purely, both regarding the language and regarding the form. I discovered in the process that he kept shifting his rhyme pattern in the quatrain he was using, and where he was unfaithful to his own precedent I followed him; even went that far. Faithful to his infidelities.

EH You were conscious of Pound's translation when doing yours.

RW I had seen it, but it was so different an effort from mine that it couldn't possibly have influenced me. At the same time I wasn't writing a rebuke to Pound—he was doing an imagist exercise upon the basis of a Voltaire poem.

EH Yes.

RW I was trying to persuade myself that I was bringing the poem alive into English with no additions of my own. I know that any such belief is an illusion, but the pursuit of the illusion can bring one closer to the fact, I think. I know that when I first tried to do some poems from the Spanish, which I don't really understand—I'm particularly prone to error when I'm doing Spanish because I know some Italian and get betrayed by cognates—even with linguistic assistance, I still manage to make blunders. When I found that I had made mistakes, I did my best to iron them out, in the light of criticism. But when the first Guillén translation was published I can remember friends saying, "That's a nice Wilbur poem, strongly influenced by Jorge Guillén." I had no such sense of it, and was distressed.

EH It might be that when you translate a contemporary this is more likely to happen. Perhaps when you translate du Bellay or Voltaire, where the language is not contemporary, the effect is different. But I wanted to ask you, in connection with what you said about Pound regarding his translation as an exercise in imagist writing, do you regard individual translations of single poems as exercises of a sort? I don't mean translations of plays now.

RW I find that I feel a kind of abhorrence for the word "exercise," even though in teaching poetry I ask my students, if they feel like it, to do this or that kind of exercise which I propose. No, I have a feeling that though I am not writing a poem of my own, I am not merely lubricating my muscles, as it were, when I bring somebody else's poem into English.

I feel as though I were doing something complete, the purpose of which lies within itself.

EH You don't feel that sense of substitution for doing your own work that Lowell talks about in his apologia for *Imitations*.

RW One or two things I've said have betrayed an awareness that I'm drawn to a poem because it's partly me and partly not me. Because to write it in English will seem to extend me emotionally. In that sense I have a personal interest in what is being done, and I am in that sense writing another poem of my own. Since I am following as carefully as I can the thoughts and feelings of someone close yet different, it's very likely going to have consequences for the next poem I write.

EH You sense that?

RW Yes.

EH As you're working or afterwards?

RW Oh, afterwards. I don't think that I would ever undertake a job of translation out of an expectation of what it would do for me as a writer, or for the purpose of keeping my hand in. But I do know, in retrospect, that by Englishing 1,800 lines of a Molière play I've doomed myself for some months thereafter to cast my thoughts in couplets—at least initially. For better or worse, ideas propose themselves in couplets for quite a while after I've done such a job.

EH Well, this then is a kind of fate—after translation. Working off a high. I spoke to John Hollander about his experiences as a translator and he mentioned Yiddish poets with whom he had to work. Because he didn't actually know Yiddish, he had to learn some and check with Irving Howe, on a poet of Russian origin named Halpern. He said this was a very significant experience for him because in doing the work he found he was able to extend his voice in such a way that after doing Halpern his own work changed—expanded in its possibilities, I take it.

RW I'm sure it's that way. Think of it on the children's playground level, where some little classmate says to you, "I dare you to say such and such a forbidden word," and you say it at once. At *his* urging. You're more capable of saying it on your own impulse thereafter.

EH So there's an extension and expansion, at least potentially, in one's work as a translator. It isn't only that one does it for pleasure, but the pleasure is really the potentiality of growing in one's own work.

RW Though I think, speaking for myself, that I would always hide any such motive from myself in the process of writing, I know that it's one of the rewards of translating.

EH Very good. I'm very interested in that. I think we should go back to the Molière plays. You did three of them.

RW Yes, and I'm now working on a fourth.[13] I didn't think I was going to do four, but I've gotten drawn into *Les femmes savantes*, and am now approaching the end of the first act. So I suppose I'll go on to the end.[14]

EH Are you doing this one in the same way you did the others?

RW Yes, and of course by now it does go faster. I know how to do it, much more surely than when I began with *The Misanthrope*, around 1952. At the same time, there are a few obstacles that arise when one is doing a fourth Molière play. Though Molière shamelessly reproduced his own rhymes and situations, I feel hesitant to use once again the same rhymes by which I solved the couplets of the other three plays I have done. That's silly, but I nevertheless feel it.

EH Are only certain rhymes possible or ideally any number of them?

RW Given a coercive text that wants you to reproduce it as exactly as possible, and given what amounts to repeated vaudeville situations, one finds that the poverty of rhyme in English becomes painful; and even though Molière has, in dealing with the same comic situations, used the same words, I find myself wishing that in my own role I didn't have to. That lengthens the task.

EH It's a fine psychological matter. I wonder if it has to do with your being a modern poet who doesn't like to repeat himself, or whether it has to do with your not being essentially a professional playwright, in the way Molière was, who would know the value of the stock and type things that work in theater.

RW I'm sure that both of those things would be true. I expect that most poets who choose to rhyme, nowadays, are troubled about using easy rhymes and are embarrassed about using their own rhymes more than once.

EH Yes.

RW It extends also, I suppose, to the whole vocabulary. I can remember Dick Eberhart saying to me once about a poem of mine that satisfied me very much, "You've used that word before!"

EH Oh, God. Like a member of the family who knows all your bad habits.

RW Yes.

EH Well, rhyme is the essence of your translations of Molière. In some way it's what makes for the dramatic element as well as keeps the poetry going. I'm not sure I'm able to explain what I mean when I say, "It makes for the dramatic element," because one would think that rhyme would *stop* dramatic happening or would be an artifice that was too transparent.

RW I think the transparency and prosaic quality of so much of the language keeps the rhyme from seeming too artificial. And also, the flow of Molière's speech, his tendency not to close every couplet, makes it possible for rhyme to attain its chief effect as provider of poetic emphasis. And also as a sign of the stages of an argument: one of the things I've noticed is that, in the very best prose translations of these verse plays of Molière, the long speeches seem infinitely too long. That is because the steps and the stages are not in the prose demarcated by measures and rhymes.

EH He has a number of long speeches.

RW Lots of *tirades*, yes.

EH I suppose that one of the things that strikes an English reader about rhyme in verse plays, where our tradition is unrhymed iambic pentameter, is the fact that in other traditions one can get so much out of a simple and very basic kind of rhyme—I mean in foreign language plays. In Spanish, for example, almost any playwright writing in Molière's time would be engaged in doing a play where there are about eight or ten different verse forms possible, and each used formulaically according to the kind of emotion or the kind of situation, usually quite stock, that is being prepared.

RW So there would be a rough analogy to grand opera.

EH Yes. But of course it's impossible to reproduce in translation, though it's been attempted in the nineteenth century. One would expect to find a greater variety in such drama, just as, I suppose, one wonders that a musical tune, a complicated one, can be played on a simple stringed instrument, which may have only one string, like the *gusle*, say. There must be something there having to do with the way the form is traditionally maneuvered.

RW   You mean that the couplet, as Molière uses it, must be a very supple form.

EH   Yes.

RW   I think it is. As he uses it, very often he will produce the equivalent of an aria. Then there will be the long speeches, recognizable as *tirades*; very often there will be stichomythia, the trading-off of couplets or of individual lines; then often there will be patterns in which people will exchange speeches of six lines in length. Very often when there is a six-line speech, it will break down into three couplets paralleling each other, repeating the thought in very much the way that the divisions of the sonnet often do. And, of course, many Molière plays break briefly into prose. A letter, for example, will be in prose.

EH   So you're pointing to the ways in which the standard couplet could be made various enough to accommodate certain changes.

RW   There are, additionally, songs and poems produced by the characters of the plays. M. Trissotin produces a horrible poem in *The Learned Ladies*.

EH   You chose to translate all four plays. You were not assigned to do them.

RW   No. I got the idea of doing *The Misanthrope* from having seen it done by the Comédie Française in 1948, and from having associations with The Poets Theatre in Cambridge, and from applying to the Guggenheims for an award which would enable me to write a poetic play. I did try to write one in New Mexico, but had no luck. It occurred to me that translating *The Misanthrope* would be a good thing to do in itself, and might teach me something about poetry in the theater. I don't think that I had any thoughts of performance when I started out. I was simply producing, I hoped, a finished reading version. And I was rather surprised, when The Poets Theatre did it in 1955, to find how satisfactorily it worked on the stage, since I had practically no experience in the theater and didn't know how to write for actors. I know that my later translations of Molière are better paced and articulated for the voices of actors and actresses than *The Misanthrope* is.

EH   So that after having stumbled on a way to make voices viable in translation, you found yourself listening to what you were doing with that consciousness, knowing that the work would be performed.

RW   Yes, as soon as The Poets Theatre started producing *The Misan-*

thrope—and then afterwards, when it was done in New York and began to be done in other places—I found myself hanging around the theater listening to people wrestling with what I'd written.

EH And then discovering surprising things, no doubt.

RW Yes, finding in some cases that I'd wrought better than I knew, and in some cases that I'd produced conjunctions of sounds that were difficult to articulate—or had, in choosing between two possible renderings of a line, taken the less dramatic way. Now I always say the lines aloud and imagine the thing in production.

EH You think that has changed the way you write?

RW Yes.

EH So that in some ways you've become a dramatist despite yourself?

RW Yes. And then, of course, all of this has had an effect upon my own poetry, which in a very general sense of the word has become more dramatic.

EH The feeling you have about the writing of your own poetry is not a stable thing—it's modified all the time by the things you want to put into it, ways you want to get them into the poetry. And translation is an avenue that's always open in some way to provide you with certain alternatives to the ways you'd been writing before.

RW Yes. It proves to be so. At the same time, as I've said, I'd never consciously use translation, as a means to something else.

EH Well, there's more to what one does than just producing something that works, isn't there? Some views of the translator and his product have it that all that counts is not any theory at all or even whether the translator knows the source language. All that matters is whether the translation works or not, and I have a feeling that's too blunt a view of what really is involved.

RW I couldn't possibly translate if I thought—what may well be true of one or two of my efforts—that the product was justified merely by its *working*. It has to work merely in a faithful way. There wouldn't otherwise seem to me to be any reason not to have written one's own poem, and there wouldn't seem to me any reason to put the name of the victimized author of the original to the translation.

EH I know you've written about this in an issue of *Translation 2*,[15] the periodical published at Columbia, but I don't recall if you said anything about an aspect of the subject that I'd like to bring up now. Poets who have translated and then have themselves been subjected to translation by others must face a unique double process of transformation. I wonder if your feelings match those of other poets I've spoken to—that the translator should produce not a slavish imitation of the work but a readable poem in his or her own language, based on your work.

RW   Well, I think there must come moments in the most faithfully intended translation when you have a choice between reproducing what is apparently, in the dictionary sense of the term, the exact meaning of the original, and falling below the aesthetic level of the rest, or providing what seems to you a close equivalent. I think that I would always go for the close equivalent in such a case. I like something that Jackson Mathews once said, when he was speaking well of my translation of *Tartuffe*. Instead of describing it as word-for-word faithful, he said that it was thought-for-thought faithful. Now if you propose to be thought-for-thought faithful, which means not leaving out any of the thoughts of the original, you can chuck particular words that don't have handsome equivalents in your own language.

EH   It's clear that translation can never be word-for-word.

RW   Even when one is translating Molière, who really *is* close to us. There are a lot of things in the English and American traditions through which you can reach out to Molière, and you can put him into a form that is oddly familiar to us, even though rhymed drama isn't part of our recent tradition.

EH   How do you feel about translating from languages you don't know, like Russian, Spanish, and Hungarian? I mean, if you have a view that you must be more faithful than not to the original text, then you must have to trust to the fact that your informant in the language you don't know is faithful.

RW   Well, for one thing, I always get a lot of information out of my informant. I spent, oh, a couple of days sitting and drinking scotch with Max Hayward while we talked over three poems only of Voznesensky's. He read over the poems to me in Russian, and he gave me, with admirable restraint, strictly prosaic translations of them, not pushing me toward one or another word choice, and I asked him questions about the appropriateness of the meters to the subject, and I asked questions about the individual Russian words—what their flavors were, whether they

were high or low—that sort of thing. I took notes all the time about what
he told me. By the time I was through, I really had done about as much
thinking (though not in the same order) as I would do in producing a
poem of my own. About as much thinking, or researching, or recogniz-
ing, or questioning. I've just translated two poems from Hungarian,
using literal versions sent me by the editors of the *New Hungarian Quarterly*, to which were appended comments on the characters and tones of
the poems, and which were accompanied also by the originals. I would
never try to translate anything without the original there—even where
I do not understand the language. Looking at the originals of these
Hungarian poems, I was able to catch something of their rhythm. I
recognized certain words, and so drew closer, or felt I was drawing
closer, to the poems themselves. And I've done the same with Spanish.
Of course, Spanish is not so forbidding a language, to someone who has
French or Italian, as Hungarian would be. Yet I have asked an intolerable lot of questions of the people who were helping me with Spanish. In
the case of Russian, I've boned up in a kind of elementary way on the language, so that at least I have leapt the hedge of the Cyrillic alphabet and
can sound the lines to myself.

EH   Do you get much from sound in Russian? Does it help in any way?

RW   A good deal. And it helps me a good deal that I've heard many
people declaim Russian poetry.

EH   Do you think if English were declaimed, in the way that Russian
conventionally is declaimed, that would similarly affect, let's say, some
hypothetical translator of Poe?

RW   It has to be Poe, doesn't it?

EH   Well, maybe Vachel Lindsay would do.

RW   Maybe Vachel Lindsay, Sidney Lanier's "Marshes of Glynn,"
maybe certain English poems. Some of Dowson or Yeats might do well if
translated by someone accustomed to the declamatory.

EH   I recall a reading where Voznesensky had worked up a way, which
is very familiar now to his audiences here, of declaiming his poems, perhaps starting with a translation in English from a reader who accompanied him on the podium, then waving the translator aside at the last
poem, and saying, "You aren't necessary now," and then speaking that
poem about the bells so the sounds came through on their own in the best
unadulterated Russian manner. Which brings up a question about the

degree of one's knowledge of, or fluency in, a foreign language. If one knows, say, French well, it's not knowing it as well as any native knows it, even if he's bilingual, as Nabokov is, or Beckett, or Borges. What is so utterly familiar to him, especially if he's a writer, seems to channel itself into one place, which is what he can get out of it as a literary trove, rather than the idiom as it flows and flows ordinarily, when one is native to the language. I'm not sure this is clear. What I'm trying to say is that perhaps there isn't finally a knowledge of a language satisfactory enough to any translator so that he can always feel certain that he knows the right thing to know.

RW   I'm sure that's true. I rather suspect that if there's an exception to your rule it would be Nabokov.

EH   Perhaps so.

RW   I remember a sentence or so in a letter of Ezra Pound's to Iris Barry. He tells her that for purposes of translation, you don't have to know all those languages. You only have to know the words in the best poems in those languages. He's being preposterous, I think. He's probably aware of a certain bravado in what he's saying, and yet there's also a certain truth in it too. He's saying what it is you are in fact likely to be working with when you do a job of translation. I suppose for someone like Borges, who speaks a very easy English, the English of Robert Louis Stevenson is more central than it is for me, say. However good his English is, it's slightly odd—it's connected with, centered in, specific literary enjoyments of his past. My knowledge of any foreign language, even if I worked harder on it than I've ever done, would continue to be so limited it would still be much more literary than that of a native.

EH   One conclusion you could come to, then, about poets translating from a foreign language is that they are crafting a thing, an object, that becomes a poem, rather than using the language as a means of communication in the usual sense. The poet-translator is creating an object apparently that will stand in place, as say, in the original French, a poem of Baudelaire's does. The communication exists in terms of the object rather than a linguistic exchange inviting an immediate interpersonal response, as in a conversation.

RW   That's right. It's the making of an object rather than the getting of something off one's chest, or the addressing of a conjectural audience out there. I think I was confessing as much a few minutes ago when I said that when I translate I am putting such abilities as I have at the service of someone else's poem in another language. Now when I write a poem of my own, I don't think I'm putting my abilities at the service of any-thing—I don't think that way then. I think in a quite strictly Emersonian way about how a poem of my own comes about. What matters is what I'm saying and the form that the poem takes is simply a part of what I'm saying. If I approach a sonnet, for example of Borges, as I dared to do several times, I have to start with a consciousness that the sonnet form must be *coped* with. I do not *elect* it.

EH   As these things go, the realization is often surprising after one has done the work. Sometimes I wonder if one isn't translating all the time—even in writing one's own poems, in a sense. I don't mean in a general way, from experience and so on, but in using a language that's totally free flowing, the idiomatic English that one speaks as we're speaking it now. . . .

RW   Yes.

EH   . . . suddenly becoming something else, transforming itself. . . .

RW   Yes, into something more condensed and precise.

EH   Yes.

RW   And then there's the translation from the preverbal. I happen to think, in the teeth of certain philosophers, that there are preverbal thoughts from which we fumblingly begin. Don't we often, well before the "idea" of a poem has begun to clarify, feel an odd certainty about the proportions of what is coming on, about its tenor, savor, stance, or mode—about the channels of logic or feeling in which it is going to run? I think of Yeats's statement that a poem often came to him first as a phrase of music. And there's a passage in Mallarmé somewhere that I may have misunderstood, but that comes to mind, in which the poet senses the awakening of a voice, perhaps his own, "Encore dans les plis jaunes de la pensée." I wonder if Aristotle, in deriving the formulae of the tragic and other emotions, may not have pointed in the direction of that speech-before-speech I'm talking about. I don't mean, for God's sake, that one makes an unconscious, abstract resolve to write a tragedy or a ballad—subject always comes first. What I mean is that the subject, before we fully know it, seems often to have done a good deal of occult marshaling.

6 / Robert Fitzgerald

EH   I suppose the justification for this conversation is that we speak together as poets who translate and not as translators who happen to be poets. What ensues here is what we will discover by talking about the subject of your work as a double agent. To begin: What motivated you to do translation? Did you start in a more or less deliberate way to be a translator?

RF   I think there are perhaps two ways in which one can begin. One would be by taking up a purely literary challenge—as at Harvard, when I was approaching the end of my senior year and needed money, and became aware of a prize given every year for the translation of one of the odes of Horace. This was an assigned ode, which I would not have chosen to translate and had no particular feeling for. I did it because I wanted two hundred dollars. That's the crude and simple example I think of as one of the ways it comes about. I did not win the prize either.

EH   That's an anticlimax!

RF   Of course the other and more serious way in which it all happens is that one finds in poems and language some quality one appropriates for oneself and wishes to reproduce. So, for years I had in my head certain lines of François Villon, which I first came across in 1931 when I was a student here at Harvard. I found the lines turning into a ballade in English in 1940, after nine years of knocking around in my head, of being heard there in French. Words began to appear in English and to make some kind of equivalent. For what satisfaction it is hard to say, except that something seems unusually piercing, living, handsome, in another language, and since English is yours, you wish it to be there too.

EH In that case there was a gestation period of nine years.

RF Yes, and almost no deliberate effort involved—just the tune beginning to play itself in English rather than in French.

EH The special sense for another language is important too. As you know, there are poets, particularly nowadays, who translate without knowing another language—the original, that is—but do it through informants. Maybe that sort of thing has always happened in some sense, but not as frequently or so much a matter of course as today.

RF I don't see how it's done, really, and wouldn't like it myself. The heart of the matter seems to me to be the direct interaction between one's making a poem in English and a poem in the language that one understands and values. I don't see how you can do it otherwise. Of course anything can happen, and as we know there are a great many examples of the other way of doing it, but I myself don't think I would enjoy it.

EH Do you suppose that's because you happen to be a man who's gifted as a speaker and reader of several languages and therefore that languages are a part of your natural background and education as a poet?

RF Well, maybe so, although I don't think I am particularly gifted in languages. In fact, oddly enough, it may have something to do with my being slow at languages. Having been rather especially slow at getting any grip on Greek, I think my wish to keep on with the struggle accounted for my doing, every few years, with Dudley Fitts to begin with, a translation of a Greek play. After leaving college and while working on a newspaper and then on a magazine in New York, I wanted not to lose what Greek I had acquired. I wanted to keep that alive in my field of vision, and so I welcomed the chance every two or three years, with Dudley, to recover the Greek, because that was necessary in each case; one loses it. That helped me to keep in touch with myself and to keep in touch with this really quite extraordinary language and literature into which I had pushed a little way.

EH I'd like to go into two of the things you mentioned. You said that you worked with Dudley Fitts to keep your Greek alive, and then that you evidently translated from French. . . . I don't want to call one language living and the other one dead, because anything you translate is living, as you yourself have said somewhere. Let's say, from a modern language as opposed to an ancient language. You translated out of both during those years before coming to the university to teach. Evidently, then, you were a translator out of two very different cultures.

RF Oh, yes. Well, with the French language, which I understood and spoke, however imperfectly, and read in great quantities, at certain times, the matter I suppose was slightly different from either Latin or Greek. One had in one's head spoken cadences. One could relate the language to something heard in France during the brief times one was there, but that was not the case with Greek. On the other hand, I was very fortunate, I believe, in this: that when I was a senior at Harvard the Classical Club put on a production of a play of Sophocles' in Greek. For this production I had to memorize six or seven hundred lines of Greek—very good Sophoclean Greek. The play was the *Philoctetes*. And if ever there was a chance to hear the language spoken I could be said to have had it then. Because there were matters of memorizing the part, of rehearsals, and finally of the production itself, which I think was repeated twice. This involved not only the dialogue in Greek iambic trimeter but the passages of Kommos, that is, exchanges between the protagonist and the chorus in choral meters. Some of that, indeed, had to be sung. All this was really a great advantage in making the language come nearer, at least to being a living one for me, than it might otherwise have been.

EH That must have been an extraordinary experience. There used to be a tradition at Harvard of putting on classical plays in the Houses. I believe everyone has heard about the *Philoctetes* performance. Do I understand that Harry Levin was in it?

RF Harry Levin was indeed in it although he had no Greek and memorized his part phonetically.[16] Henry Hatfield was in it. Milman Parry was the director. Mason Hammond was on hand, and John Finley helped to coach the chorus in the choral meters. The music for it was extremely impressive: it was done by Elliott Carter, who had been here a year or two before and was at that point in Paris studying with Nadia Boulanger. He was induced to make quite beautiful music for the chorus.

EH A very unusual occasion and cast—and production probably.

RF I think that everyone who took part has always been grateful for it.

EH Well, there may be something in this related to my other question about your working with Dudley Fitts. That is, in your experience as a translator, your basic sense of the languages and the fact of participating with others helped in sort of bringing it all forth and in keeping it going.

RF Yes, sure.

EH Translation is not done simply in the way that one writes poetry oneself—at a desk in a closed room, with the traffic of the world shut out. Is there anything here that would interest you to comment on?

RF Well, what it was like. I think it was the summer after I left Harvard. Dudley and I stopped at a performance—somewhere at a girls' school in New England—one of Euripides' plays in a version by Gilbert Murray. We were dissatisfied, to say the least, with what we heard and saw, and I guess on talking it over afterward we more or less lightly said to one another, "Why couldn't *we* try it?" From this there came the first collaboration, on the *Alcestis* of Euripides. We worked of course separately, sending drafts back and forth and occasionally getting together to talk it over. I don't remember in detail how it all worked out. But after it was done, and likewise just for fun, we showed it to someone we knew who was working at Harcourt Brace. And Harcourt Brace published it. Edith Hamilton remarked it was the best translation of a Greek play she'd ever read. That was very heartening and very surprising, and there we were. It had been a pleasant experience and we tried it again, with the *Antigone* of Sophocles, a few years later. Then, when I was in Santa Fe, New Mexico, in 1940, I did a translation of the *Oedipus at Colonus* of Sophocles. I had been moved by the play when I first read it as an undergraduate. And I had always thought possibly of trying to handle it and others in English, being really intensely dissatisfied with the English versions of these things that existed. That was part of it: the overpowering sense that justice had not been done to the poetry of Sophocles and that something approaching justice might not be so difficult in view of the abysmal quality to our ears of what existed.

EH In both cases, as an actor in a play and as a translator, you were propelled by a sense of the dramatic elements in the work. I mean, it was not lyric poetry or, as later, narrative and epic poetry, but rather these dramatic plays . . . involving voices, the voices of characters.

RF Yes, living voices in a living language, so it seemed to us.

EH In speaking to Richard Wilbur about how he came to do Molière and about those excellent translations of his that resulted, I asked whether he had to become a dramatist in spite of himself. He thought that that was exactly true. He had first tried writing poetic plays but had given that up as a bad job. Then, during the Poets Theatre period in Cambridge in the fifties, it was his being forced by the exigencies of making Molière come alive in English, especially in working out those couplets, which seemed to be the secret of his becoming a good dramatist-translator.

RF   Of course, of all living rhymers Dick is the most accomplished; he has a genius for rhyme and meter. I love what he said in the foreword to his version of *Tartuffe*—that as translator he could claim as his main virtue patience, the patience of waiting until the lines are right—this beautiful virtue of a good poet.

EH   It seems, perhaps in some other way, that poets find another voice, or the possibility of another voice, when they translate, more vividly, even more spectacularly than when they're doing their own poems. This too is a dramatic thing.

RF   Yes, I suppose that's part of the interest and excitement of doing translation, that it does give you personae, as they say, and takes you out of your lyric self.

EH   What *does* occur when you become aware of what is happening? These are tricky questions and I'm not sure I know how to ask them. Obviously a relationship exists between the impulse to translate and the impulse to do one's own poems, and, in each instance, also, between lyric poetry that's translated and the translation of poetic drama. Now, is there also a way in which the activity of translating extends the range of one's poetic voice as a poet? Does it affect your own poetry? Did you notice that?

RF   I don't know how to answer that. There must of course be a relationship between translating and making poems of your own, but what it is I just don't know. I guess I tend to think of the two activities not as they are often referred to, as closely allied, but rather as very distinct. If you are a poet or aspire to be one, the inference is that when you translate you are embodying that kind of effort simply in another form. I wonder. I don't think it's quite so simple, and I feel very hesitant to commit myself to what I think one does hear often as the version of what happens— that is, that a poet is always doing the same thing, or a disguised form of it, in translation. I don't think that's true. I think that one poet is lending himself to the other poet, that the obligation is to the other poet, and that one is taking on for the time being the spirit and impulse and intent of the other poet, and so the wish is to make all that clear in one's own language rather than express oneself, so to speak.

EH   What you say sounds very like a statement Dick Wilbur made. His view is that the translator serves the poet being translated, and the service done is exclusively to bring the foreign work across into the other language.

RF That I think I agree with.

EH There are many sides to this matter. As you say, one involves the idea of persona. A persona both masks and amplifies, in the sense of giving focus and range to, the actor; it both reveals and disguises him. I think that double function can be applied to poetic translation too.

RF Well, maybe so. Of course in taking on, as I put it, the poetic being that is out there, one is perhaps acquiring another personage for oneself. But the sense one has of it is not so much that one is appropriating something as that one is suiting another and putting one's gifts, whatever they are, at his disposal in order that what he did shall become an English thing.

EH Isn't that related to the other impulse you mentioned before when with Dudley Fitts you saw a production of that Euripides play? You were both dissatisfied and sensed that a disservice had been done by the translation.

RF Right. We were dissatisfied on his behalf, so to speak.

EH One tries, then, in some way, to correct a mistaken impression by retranslating something that has been done imperfectly or poorly.

RF In a way you can feel that the poet actually is looking over your shoulder, and you say to yourself, now, how would this go for him? Would this do or not? And that, I think, is leading us pretty close to the heart of the matter. I have an example that I'm very fond of, in one of Richard Wilbur's translations of Villon. It is "The Ballade of the Dead Ladies." It begins,

> Dites-moi où, n'en quel pays,
> Est Flora, la belle Romaine,
> Archipiades ni Thäis,
> Qui fut sa cousine germaine. . . .

Oh, "Tell me where, on lands or seas, / Flora the Roman belle has strayed, / Archipiades or Thäis, / Who put each other in the shade." Now, the French says of the second of these dead lovelies—two courtesans, as he understood them—that she was the *cousine germaine* of the first. In what respect was she a first cousin? She was first cousin in re-

spect to her beauty. Now Wilbur found in English idiom a lovely phrase
for what one beauty does to another beauty. She puts her in the shade, if
she can, and he translates that line, "who put each other in the shade"—
literally utterly remote from the French. But, my point is that had Villon
been using our language, and had he found that idiom, that same phrase,
he would have been delighted to use it in that place.

EH Yes, indeed.

RF His job being to make a ballade, a rhymed composition, with lines
that would of course make sense, that was the nature of what he was doing, and Wilbur, to my mind perfectly, exemplifies one of the principles
of good translation.

EH That's a fine example having to do with the nature of lyric poetry.
You can extend the principle to any poetry that rhymes and is not necessarily lyric but dramatic: that the right conjunction of words must be
sought and found, words in perhaps a more extended form, as in narrative poetry. This isn't the main point of such poetry, but then you're the
authority on narrative poetry—Homer, in this regard.

RF Well, I would then go on to say that Homer, as we now know,
was working in what they call an oral tradition. Now the performer—
because that's what he was—had at his disposal a great repertory of
themes, narrative and dramatic situations, and he had at his disposal
a great repertory of formulae, of lines, half lines, phrases, all metrical, let
it be observed, that could be modified or used in many contexts during
his performance, which was always to some extent extemporary. Now,
as he went along with his tale, he could and did invent new ways of
handling episodes and passages that made each performance, in some
way, a new thing. Do you see how this fact liberates, to a certain extent,
the translator?

EH Yes.

RF If his obligation as I have thought is always to the originator, to the
original imagination, then he knows that for that imagination no text, no
text sacred or otherwise, existed, that free improvisation was part of the
essence of each performance. Therefore, what is known as freedom in
translation would be nearer to what the original performer expected of
a translator than it might be in the case of someone who had, like say Paul
Valéry, labored over every line and for whom the final text in every detail had more importance than for the Homeric singer.

EH   Your emphasis makes me understand the term "poetic license" in an entirely different way. The slightly pejorative sense of the phrase suddenly seems to have another meaning.

RF   Yes, one sees by virtue of this slight liberation that in fact all works of imagination are improvisation at some stage, at the beginning certainly. And one sees how precious this sheer invention is in the making of a work of art. I remember at a certain point in working on the *Odyssey* that Rudyard Kipling's stories, which I was reading, as it happened, to my children in Italian versions, reminded me of the possibilities of sheer invention. In one of the stories there is a seal, who is the hero, and his life is spent in the oceans of the world. He has as part of his private language phrases and exclamations that refer to his life as a seal in the great cold South Atlantic waters, like swearing "by the foaming straits of Magellan." I can't recall now—I wish I could—some of the language that Kipling invented for his seal, but all of this is important, it seems to me, in the imaginative field of someone working on something so tremendously inventive as the Homeric poems. If you think that someone was able to invent those actions and sustain them and elaborate them over such a span with such constant resources of surprise, dramatic scene-making, and dramatic language, then I think the interest that this kind of consideration has will not seem too remote.

EH   That may relate to something I was thinking in reading your translations. It's the supposition that in being aware of the oral tradition behind the compositions, the kind of performance-invention you just described, you become the first translator of Homer who consciously used it in working out a variety of possibilities in voice and characterization.

RF   Well, to some extent maybe that's true, but one may imagine that in the future, as this understanding deepens and widens, more appropriate forms may be found for it. I'd say I made a beginning.

EH   A very important one. But you seem also to bring with it as a principle something that belies the idea that there are only two possibilities in writing poetry: writing in closed and writing in open forms—that is, free verse as against metered and rhymed verse—by indicating that with a consciousness of all traditions, one's sense of the techniques of verse, meter, and sound becomes indeed a tool by which one finds the freedom to write or to perform and invent through translation.

RF   Let's bring our talk back to earth a little and remember that what the translator—myself in particular—does is not comparable to what the Homeric performer was doing. His art was comparable to the art of the great musical virtuoso who can improvise, who can sit at the piano and by his mastery, both of the performing technique and of the musical background, can make music. The translator—and I now think of my own sweating days and nights—does one draft after another; he's a sedentary craftsman trying through repeated trials and failures to arrive at a readable English page. I did it by writing out the Greek of each book in a ledger-type notebook: each Greek line followed by two blank lines. While I did this, I would use the dictionary and what scholarship I could find to clear up puzzles in the text. When I went to work I had nothing but my own Greek in my own hand before me to try to match with English in the blank lines underneath the Greek. Then the typewritten drafts began, and every evening I would destroy half of what I had done every morning, and often a day's work would be only a few lines. I had from the beginning a sense that I didn't care how long it took and if I had to wait a week for a suitable version of one exclamation I would wait a week and, you know—no hurry. Patience. Patience. Dick Wilbur's quality.

EH Yes. We *have* been brought down to earth. What I had in mind was perhaps this: that whatever we discover that's useful—as you did, presumably, through Milman Parry—about the oral tradition of Homeric performance-invention, our task is still not analogous but rather, because we're literate and writing people, our consciousness is wider, say, than the consciousness of Pope in his renditions of Homer. I would imagine that that's one difference.

RF One mustn't underrate Pope. His notes to his translations are extraordinarily perceptive and sharp. One should indeed read Pope with his notes available, in the Twickenham edition possibly, to see what a vast amount he did understand about Homer. Given the scholarship of his time, it's extraordinary how penetrating and sensitive a good deal of his understanding was. In his case one does again have the sense that of course for him it was a text, and it was a text that he came to through Latin. The Roman or Latin tradition was very strong in his interpretation of Homer, so that one can find passages in his *Iliad* that are directly indebted to Dryden's *Aeneis*, for example; that was his immediate exemplar. He greatly admired what Dryden had done and in his way was doing the same thing. So the Vergilian tinge and the Roman tinge in English Augustan understanding of Greek is very perceptible in Pope.

EH   As Ben Brower put it, Pope's *Iliad* will probably never go unread; that is, it will always be read as a permanent work. But as for relying on one's precursors—as Pope on Dryden—does anything like it apply to your translation? Did you have a sense of dependence on other efforts?

RF   Not at all. I'd say that there was a conscious attempt to take the Greek unmediated by Latin and, even in such minor matters as the transliteration of proper names, to insist upon the Hellenistic quality of the poem and to avoid Latinizations. The question has another aspect, however, and that is that our own language has its Latin component: it's impossible to avoid Latinism in English. In fact, eloquence in English will inevitably make use of the Latin element in our vocabulary. At the same time, I feel—and I guess this has been noticed about the translations I've done—that the strength of our language comes largely from the Anglo-Saxon and the Old English (Old Germanic parts of it), and I think there was a conscious effort to make use of those simplicities and that force in the work.

EH   So when we speak of relying on precursors—wasn't it Borges who said that every poet invents his own precursors?—I wonder if we couldn't add to the idea of the text the fact of others working at the same text—and by extension, also, of the landscape or seascape, as with Homer you apparently did, according to your notes referring to Ithaca, the search for Ithaca and the islands—all being part of the total effort and research to establish the text.

RF   Yes, well there again, the work of the imagination originally came out of a particular air that blew over a particular body of water.

EH   Wind puffs, you called them.

RF   Yes, and there were changes of light on landscapes and changes of direction of the wind and the force of the wind and weather. That whole scene is too important in Homer to neglect. I think it was lucky that during most of the work on the *Odyssey* I lived on Homer's sea in houses that were, in one case, shaken by the impact of the Mediterranean winter storms on the rocks below, and the constant visual presence of those seascapes may have had something to do with the way in which that poem came to be.

EH   I'm very impressed by the relation between place and poetic invention. I was conscious of it in my own work and, similar to your experience, remember that, for example, when I was doing some translations of Cervantes, I was reading newspapers in Mallorca—I was doing the *entremeses*, and I think there's a reference in them—though I may be wrong because the reference may really be in the *Novelas ejemplares*—to the flood that annually overflows the banks of the Guadalquivir in Seville. So, while working on Cervantes there in Mallorca I was reading an account in the paper of the same flood happening then, in 1958. There was a certain sense in which my being there—say, the livingness of the moment of my job—made a bridge between Cervantes' text and my bringing his words over into English.

RF That's wonderful.

EH This being in touch with various sources—and the more the better—also applies in your case to the extremely close reading you gave the Homeric poems and all the scholarship on them, which becomes part of your effort. Now, in connection with the language you use there's something I want to ask, and that is, about the very convention of formulaic and epithetical phrases, which is based on repetition and, like rhyme, intended to ring a bell in the listener's ear. But this convention is also antithetical nowadays, let's say to modern ears or in modern poetry where one avoids repeating sounds. How do you cope with that problem in your translations?

RF Yes, the question is a very large one because it involves the relationship, not between one style and another but between one whole language and another: Homer's whole language, the language in which he lived, the language that he breathed, because he never saw it, or certainly those who formed his tradition never saw it, in characters on the pages. It was all on the tongue and in the ear. This was all formulaic, by its very nature. The phrase was the unit, you could say, rather than the word. There were no dictionaries and no sense of vocabulary such as we have. Now, the language that had grown up and formed itself on those principles is what one is dealing with, and the problem is to bring a work of art in that medium into another medium formed on different principles and heard and understood in a different way. So it's really a larger question than merely the question of whether one is to reproduce in some standard form formulaic expressions in Greek by formulaic expressions in English. The question is how to bring a work of imagination out of one language that was just as taken-for-granted by the persons who used it as our language is by ourselves. Nothing strange about it. So to make something that *is* strange to our ears would not be doing justice to the work that was not strange to theirs.

EH   I think you put that very vividly. What seems almost impossible is the task of bringing the effect of the original work, a work intended for oral performance, into another language where the tradition is literary—or somehow to preserve the amenities of both kinds of language, oral and written, together.

RF   I suppose one hopes—you know, as I hoped and hope—that these would be readable to people who would only read them. But I have also—and repeatedly in reading them aloud—made the point that they were originally meant to be heard and were heard, and I happily, not too long ago, made two recordings: one of passages from the *Odyssey* and one of the two books of the *Iliad*, and both are now being produced and marketed in the Yale Series of Recorded Poets, so that my readings of these things, at any rate, are hearable as well as readable.

EH   Yes, that's very valuable and very good that you have put it on records. Projecting it by voice is what makes the poem come alive. In your notes, your reference to the instrument that the performing poet used as an accompanying sound, or as part of the performance to go along with the voice, made me think that such a convention would not be strange to a guitar-playing Bob Dylan, mainly in the sense that the two things go together.

RF   Right, right. The invention of Bob Dylan with his guitar belongs in its way to the same kind of tradition of something meant to be heard, as the songs of Homer.

EH   The difference, one has to say—or let me just say it for myself—is that one is so often disappointed with what it looks like on the page after one has heard it with one's ears.

RF   That's right.

EH   There seems to be that hiatus between the performance and the written record.

RF   That's right. And of course, too, all the dramatic and narrative interest, or a lot of it—the kind of lyric and dramatic interest in Homer—is a different thing from what one has in these songs. Still, that they are inventive and that they do make use of several available traditions, hillbilly tradition, folk tradition, and that they are sophisticated—

because of course the Homeric poems were intensely so—all this I think amounts to a resemblance. Maybe a slight one, but there it is.

EH Are you personally interested in the kind of poetry that young people are writing today? (That's not a "political" question!) I mean, sensitive to the values that may be emerging from poetry dedicated to oral rather than written traditions.

RF Sure. I would be inconsistent if I were not.

EH I put it that way because often the results are disappointing, as the verses of Dylan often seem.

RF Yes. I feel that disappointment very often and still I find the performance often very congenial.

EH Do you suppose we could go back now to what we were saying before about your preparations for doing Homer, your scholarship and so on?

RF Well, I was saying that as far as scholarship is concerned, I could not claim to be a Greek scholar. I never got an advanced degree and I never did the work that one does for an advanced degree. Academically, I'm in the English Department here and in the Department of Comparative Literature. In doing the work on Homer I began with the Oxford text and the Greek dictionary. That was my entire equipment, and it remained my entire equipment for almost a year. Then in Athens—in fact, when I visited Greece for the first time—I found several books that I thought would be extremely useful. They turned out to be Lorimer's book on Homer and the Monuments (a great study of the archaeological material with reference to Homer) and Stanford's annotated edition of the *Odyssey*. Of course I got these at once and began using them. I got Autenreith's Homeric dictionary and I subscribed to the quarterly of the American School in Athens. I began—as I went along, really—looking into and making use of the scholarship that was available. When the Ventris and Chadwick decipherment of Linear B came out I got that book from Cambridge and read it and in fact found several points extremely interesting and useful. For example, here's a case in point. Throughout the *Odyssey*, Nestor has an epithet, which is usually translated "warder of the Achaians," and no one ever knew just what that might have meant. Well now, Nestor's kingdom was on the western shore of the Peloponnesus, and the tablets from Pylos, which was his palace and capital, yielded among the categories of court retainers and servants, and so on, a category of coast watchers. It was easy then to see that, piracy being what it was in those centuries, for a well-regulated government in Pylos coast watchers were necessary. I then thought about the coastal command during the hostilities of 1939 to 1945, where, for the protection of convoys approaching the British Isles, Catalina flying boats and destroyers and destroyer escorts were organized to survey those sea approaches. The command bore the title of the Western Approaches and the commanding officer was known, I believe, as the Lord of the Western Approaches, and I then saw immediately that this was what Nestor was. He was Lord of the Western Approaches to Achaia— and there was my formula for him.

EH Yes, that's fascinating. Something slightly analogous may be the sense I picked up in Spain about contraband. Its indulgence and continued practice, going back hundreds and hundreds of years, together with its reliance on piracy and slavery, and still going on in some form while I was doing the Cervantes *entremeses* there, made me think that for a country whose civilization was built up around the traffic of the sea there is a very special and enduring series of—well, what can one say, patterns and signs?

RF Patterns and signs, yes. Here it seemed to me there was a real link between the sea raiders of the twelfth century B.C. when, as the poems themselves show, a man made his living as a sea raider often enough, and the title given to Nestor in the Homeric poems.

EH That's a very good footnote.

RF An example of how scholarship came in.

EH The other part of it is that though you are not a professional scholar by—let's say—university training, you nevertheless took on all of the work that a professional scholar would have to know and do.

RF Well, I didn't at least consciously put any value on ignorance, and I wanted to know as much as I possibly could about it all.

EH Now, if I can go on to one or two of the questions I've scribbled down to ask you, I'd be pleased to have you consider them. I was speaking with Ben Belitt about Lowell's "imitations," and it happens that Belitt has written an article about the subject. It's in the magazine *Salmagundi*. The question is the propriety of what Lowell does in taking "sudden leaps," as Belitt calls them. That is, Lowell goes along faithfully up to a point, then suddenly decides that it's rather boring, and cuts off in the process of faithful translation and introduces new material. I think this is not uncommon. I have noticed that Roy Campbell does the same thing in translating Calderón's plays and I am sure that Edward FitzGerald did this even more in his Calderón translations. After noting this, Belitt goes on to say that Lowell is nevertheless probably more faithful in his "imitations" than Pope and Dryden were in theirs. I wonder what your view might be.

RF   Well, my feeling is that Lowell was fully justified in doing what he did and calling it not translation but "imitation." It warns the reader that what he is about to read is not a version of the original but something in the nature of a collaboration between Cal Lowell and another poem in a different language. I would distinctly differentiate what I was trying to do from such practice. I remember before I began doing the *Odyssey*, I called on Ezra Pound at St. Elizabeth's. At that point I was thinking that the way to do it would be to hit the high spots, to translate what I could translate, so to speak, and let the rest go. I said this to Pound, and he said, "Oh no, let Homer say everything he wanted to say."

EH   Yes, although Pound "hit the high spots" in his work very often. He's done it both ways, I guess.

RF   Yes, but this was his distinct opinion, that Homer should be allowed, as he put it, to say everything he had to say, and *that* I tried to do.

EH   Well, *how* you did it, the special force of your translation, is the next thing I wanted to bring up. Up to now, our impression of Homer and Vergil as epic poets seems to have been formed for us largely by what we call the neoclassical writers and the traditions identified with Pope and Dryden, perhaps even with Chapman and Ben Jonson. Formed, that is, by them specifically in neoclassic rather than in romantic dress, in English. I'm not sure this is true in German, where perhaps the demarcations aren't as sharp—because you think of Goethe, for instance, as being both romantic and neoclassical, actually the fount of a lot of ancient classical learning and poetry. But it seems true that we don't see Greek and Latin poems through, say, romantic eyes, but through Augustan and neoclassical eyes. My point would then be that a significant result of your labors and inspiration has been to make a new dispensation available in the continuity of literary traditions. What the romantics didn't do and Robert Fitzgerald did do was to offer an alternative to the neoclassical Homer in English.

RF   Yes. Just how one would describe the alternative I would have to leave to others, but that it is an alternative I am sure I felt from the start. That is, I wished what I did to come directly from the Greek without any mediation through Latin. That was one thing. And then, I felt that couplets were highly inappropriate for Homer and that while one can read Pope with enjoyment for the simple skill and force of what he did in couplets, I doubt that one can derive from a reading of Pope anything like the narrative and dramatic life that the Homeric poems in fact have. So, I would have said, I guess, that I was trying to do something more just to the Homeric poems than the neoclassic glory gave.

EH   When we speak of Homer's *Iliad* and the *Odyssey* in the academy we assume that what we read *is* Homer, except, say, in the case of Pope's *Iliad*, where it is *Pope's Iliad* and we are conscious that Pope intervenes. But with most translations of European classics—Dostoevski, the Russian novel, say—we don't bother to take the translator into account. So that now, to all effects and purposes, you are Homer, unless you are *Fitzgerald's Iliad* and *Fitzgerald's Odyssey*. This is the phenomenon I was thinking of as part of what lies behind the matter of a modern alternative. The modern Homer would have to constitute a different dispensation; students reading Homer in your two poems, your translations, would be having a very different experience from the one that we as students had in reading, say—what was it, Palmer?

RF   Palmer, yes.

EH   I don't know if that calls for a comment from you.

RF   Well, another footnote I might add here is that by the sheer accident of skipping my freshman year in high school, I never read Palmer, and I never read any translation of Homer, in fact, before I read Homer in Greek. By accident or luck, my first acquaintance with Homer was reading the *Odyssey*, slowly indeed, after I had had two years of Greek here.

EH   Well, that's all to the good, considering the strong ingredients that go into your particular work. All of them nonpredictable, unpredictable.

RF   And I would say that I did the work without really very much prior acquaintanceship with the neoclassic or any other translation.

EH   Yes, and that's very refreshing for us and very promising for readers to come. I think we can end on that good note.

Michael Astor

7 / Max Hayward

EH Let me start by asking some questions about your work as an informant to translators. The word *informant* has an oblique meaning, but that may not be to the point. In this instance, it's the work you've done in helping American poets who have little or no knowledge of Russian to bring over the poetry of the contemporary Russian poets. To begin, may I ask, is there some compatibility between Russian and English?

MH I don't think there's much compatibility, though that hasn't figured as a problem. The problems have been simply of the fact that, as you know, Russia is a very different culture and civilization. The situation of a poet in Russia is quite different from that in the Western world, obviously. Beyond the young ones, who may not like being involved, like Voznesensky, there's the dimension of sharing in a kind of civic engagement, however unpolitical they may seem to be. This is, of course, appreciated to some extent by American poets. (I've worked only with American poets.) They do understand the business of being embattled—something that the English poets lived through during the thirties in a different context. But I think the poets in your country do feel very much more part of a kind of almost oppositional movement. I may be wrong about that.

EH Let's say that in view of the political contention between the two countries, American poets would like to do something of a good turn by translating the Russian poets and in that way humanize the bleak combative politics. Which poets did you work with?

MH I worked in New York with Auden, who I somehow began to feel was an American poet. He was settled in New York then. I worked with people like Stanley Kunitz, William Jay Smith, and Richard Wilbur. There was always the feeling on their part of a sympathy and, as you say, perhaps a feeling that they were helping, and they had perhaps more understanding than some other poets would have.

EH Do you think that English translators have had any effect, literary or political, on the Russian people of the literati? Does the fact that their poets are translated into English by good poets have an effect of any sort?

MH Oh well, an enormous effect. I mean it's far more important to them to be translated than it is for Western poets to be translated into Russian. There's no question of that because it helps them in a very direct way. They've felt terribly isolated. Most of the poets presently alive in Russia, and the young ones mainly—Voznesensky and Yevtushenko—still remember the days of almost total isolation from the West. So that to be brought to a world audience—the effect of being translated into English—means more than one can possibly express.

EH There may be other implications, and maybe we'll come to those. The three best-known Russian poets in America, Brodsky, Yevtushenko, Voznesenky, were able to leave Russia (Brodsky permanently), and so have participated in the process of being translated. They have gotten to know their American counterparts and have also written about it.

MH Yes, and some have reciprocated, it's true, by translating the poets who've translated them. Wilbur's been translated by several of them. I'm trying to think now . . . Kunitz has been translated by one Soviet poet.

EH When did good English translations from Russian start being made, and by whom?

MH Well, in prose, of course, there's quite a tradition. Probably the English translations of the Russian classics were some of the first. Russian was translated earlier into French. Prosper Mérimée translated Pushkin into French and some of Turgenev, I think. But the English probably came in second as translators of Russian. And I suppose those of Constance Garnett are classical.

People tend to look down on her translations, but I think it's very unfair. She did an immense amount. She did almost all the Russian classics. She did most of Dostoevski, most of Turgenev. She did Gogol. (She worked with a Russian informant, although I think she knew some Russian. And she had a sense of literature.) And these, I think, are still very readable. She also, of course, made an idiom, which again people tend to look down at now as being too quaint. She tended to follow the Russian a little too closely. But many people still prefer her translations. Her translations of Chekhov, for instance, are often preferred to the more recent ones, which are certainly better in every respect—more accurate, and fall in more with modern colloquial English.

EH But her Russian was self-taught, wasn't it?

MH She knew it to some extent, but it was, I don't think, enough to translate it independently. She came from a literary family. This is what is important after all. I mean, to have this flair for literature is very important to the translator.

There was another good English translator called Aylmer Maude, who translated Tolstoy. He's excellent. I don't think he's as well known as she is. He translated only Tolstoy. Well, that was during the Edwardian period, and I suppose their translations were the best. I mean, since then there's been no one to compare with those two, in the scope of what they did and the influence they had.

EH And in poetry—there hasn't been that much done from the Russian—of that caliber and scope, as you say.

MH I'm afraid not. But of course it's terribly difficult. I must say I've seen very little translation of Russian poetry into English that carries any weight. It's partly because there's a great incompatibility between the languages as such. I mean, I'm convinced it's very, very hard to translate from a highly inflected language like Russian, with a mobile word order that is very plastic and so on, into a language like English, which is very rigid and poor in rhyme. Russian is terribly rich in rhyme. And it just cannot be done. Pushkin notoriously has never succeeded in English. I think there have been some very competent versions—most recently one by Walter Arndt that's very good.

EH Of which Pushkin work?

MH He translated *Eugene Onegin*.

EH And that's what Nabokov did too.

MH Yes, but that of course is a literal version. . . .

EH Sort of museum piece.

MH . . . and not a translation, I think, that one can read with pleasure. But the important things about it are his notes and explanations and whatnot, but one can't regard it as a facilitating translation.

EH Now, to go back to the contemporary Russian poets: How do you feel about the English translations—particularly in the cases where you've been involved as the informant? Say with Auden, Wilbur, Kunitz, Smith.

MH Well, in all these cases it worked very much better than I would have thought. I was frankly very skeptical of the whole idea. It wasn't my idea. It was suggested to me by somebody else who was editing the Voznesensky volume with me—Patricia Blake. And I didn't think it would work, but in fact it did very much better than I would have thought. I think the versions in the Voznesensky volume are probably as good as one could hope for, given the inherent limitations of the exercise, which is entirely due to the skill of these poets and their ability to understand not just the individual poems but the poet as such. They took great trouble and were very interested, and obviously enjoyed doing it, and did it very much as a labor of love.

EH There are certain conditions governing this matter of doing a translation from a language that one may know slightly or not at all. Among the Americans, did any know or have a sense of Russian?

MH No, none of them. None of them knew any Russian, or knew any other Slavic language. Kunitz has some slight sense of it. I think he has a Russian-speaking cousin. There is Russian in the family and so his ear, perhaps, was slightly more attuned.

EH They've all translated from other languages.

MH Wilbur has. Wilbur has translated from French. Auden has translated from the Scandinavian languages and from German, I imagine. I mean some of them certainly had experience at translating, I think as direct translators, not working with informants.

EH Which brings up a question, partly related to a view that you're acquainted with. It was recently expressed by Robert Fitzgerald during a conversation I had with him about translating from languages that one does not know well. He's so convinced that one has to know the language one is translating from, that he wouldn't comment beyond indicating that such was his view. He's a great admirer of Wilbur's French translations. And yet Wilbur, in a sense, has in some way unwittingly betrayed Fitzgerald's point of view. He has not only translated from Russian but also from Hungarian and Spanish, languages he doesn't know. When I spoke with Wilbur he explained that though he didn't know Spanish he knew Italian. They are cognate languages. And with Russian, as he told me, he learned the Cyrillic alphabet.

So now there's the view represented by Robert Fitzgerald, that one must indeed know the language one is translating from, and there's the view, say of Robert Lowell, which is that what one is doing is not a translation so much as an imitation. I have read (and wonder if you have too) Guy Daniels's article about Lowell's mistranslation of an Anna Akhmatova poem, which presumably shocked and angered the poet. Daniels refers to this practice as an example of the damage that can be done when one monkeys around with the original. What do you think?

MH Well, it's very hard to generalize. I think if one proclaims beforehand that one is doing an imitation, a *Nachdichtung*, as the Germans would say, and you make it quite plain that you just use the original as a launching pad for something of your own, I imagine that is almost legitimate. Possibly if you fall too wide of the original then it's unfair to keep the original author's name. Or you should put your own name on it, or in some way say, "inspired by the poem by Akhmatova." It would really depend on the degree to which you diverge. But of course many important translations have been extremely free and there are plenty of examples of that. I was told that what's-his-name's version of Omar Khayyám is very far removed in its relation to the original.

EH Edward—yes, the other—FitzGerald!

MH It's obviously a very successful poem in English. So that it can be very hard to generalize on that matter. As regards whether a translator should always know the original—well, ideally I would say yes. I think this is obvious. The ideal is that a great poet should translate from a language he knows very well. And there are examples of this too—as in my experience, Pasternak's versions of Shakespeare. He did know English; he worked directly from the original. And he knew German and translated Goethe's *Faust*. And these are works of genius. But this doesn't happen very often and one has to settle, obviously, in many cases, for the lower form of it—the poet working through an intermediary.

I must also say that I think here—to take up Robert Fitzgerald's point—I think that it probably depends very much on the scope of the work. I would say that this business of going through an intermediary is all right occasionally, with a small number of poems that happen to have caught the fancy of the poet. But, to undertake a major work, say all of *Faust* or all of the *Aeneid*, without knowing the original, particularly

I think if it's a classical language where there are enormous problems of interpretation and exegesis, then Fitzgerald is absolutely right. Because he is talking from the point of view of a classical scholar, of one who has translated all of Homer, and I would agree with him in this case. It would be very, very difficult to do without the original. I don't even think anybody would dream of attempting it. There are very good translations of very long classical works. These can only be done, obviously, by people who are both scholars and poets. The translation of Vergil—by Mandelbaum, is it?

EH   Yes, Allen Mandelbaum.

MH   Mandelbaum's would show this—as much of it as I looked at was very good, superbly done. It could only have been done by a classical scholar with his particular interests.

EH   Perhaps the case of Robert Fitzgerald is unique, since without being a professional academic scholar of Greek he's kept up his Greek since college and he's also been a poet. Actually, he's had a career in journalism, and I think the translation is what kept him going.

MH   He has obviously been at work on it. He has reverted to his classical studies, and one can see that he's wrestled with problems of scholarship. I mean you have to make choices quite often in Homer between different possibilities or hypotheses about certain passages. And you can only do this in an informed way if you are capable of reading the original in a scholarly way.

EH   In this connection I wonder if you are aware of a rather acerbic review that Fitzgerald's *Odyssey* got from Donald Carne-Ross in the *New York Review of Books*. Carne-Ross was disappointed with Fitzgerald's translation, and compared it with another translation, done by the English poet Christopher Logue.

MH   Yes, I saw the article.

EH   As you know, then, Carne-Ross says in effect, here's a translator who does a better job with a free adaptation or imitation, and is not a Greek scholar.

MH   Yes, I saw the quotations from the Logue versions. . . . Well, it's all a matter of taste.

EH   Is there something perverse about it all?

MH   I mean the quotations didn't strike me as being superior to Fitzgerald's.

EH Perhaps in this case it's the principle Carne-Ross favors—the Poundian principle of "make it new." And that's what makes him prefer the Logue to the Fitzgerald version.

MH Well, it's perhaps getting us off the subject, but I think this problem of translating long epics and ancient ones, such as Homer and Vergil, into modern English, is a very difficult one, partly because the genre no longer exists. You can have epic poems in eighteenth-century English but cannot sustain the translation in any form nowadays. People have tried every possible formula, including prose translations, which of course fall intolerably flat. I think Fitzgerald's is probably a good kind of compromise. He's not trying to follow some rigid epic pattern but produces a flexible modern English that is still recognizably some kind of poem.

EH Fine, if it has the savor of a poem.

MH It has the savor of a poem. I think Lattimore's versions are very good too for a modern reader. But it's a hopeless exercise.

EH Absolutely hopeless?

MH I think it's an absolutely hopeless exercise. I don't think it can be done in prose or verse.

EH And there's the additional impossibility, as you say, of epic not being a viable modern form, so that one abruptly confronts both a formal and a linguistic problem.

MH Yes. You just cannot expect a modern reader to accept such a narrative framework. It doesn't make any sense to him, the sort of general reader you aim at. Of course, this is also the trouble with Pushkin's *Eugene Onegin*—having a novel in verse of that length in modern English is intolerable.

EH Because there's no tradition for it in English at all?

MH Not that I know of. Oh well, of course there's Byron—to some extent.

EH And Browning.

MH Yes, and Browning. But these are not really for the modern stomach, are they? Do people still read all of Byron's epics?

EH I avoided reading them, even in college—yes, and I thought I was spending my time better by reading MacNeice's *Autumn Journal*, which, come to think of it, is a sort of epic.

MH   I mean everybody knows snatches of *Don Juan* but who's going to read the whole thing now? To sit down and read it is very hard.

EH   To come back to the translations that you've had to do with as an informant: among the Russian poets, who would you say is closest to the English idiom? Or, if it comes to the same thing, who is the best translated of them?

MH   Well, I think Brodsky has been very well translated in the Penguin collection by George Kline. (The preface is by Auden.) Kline is a Russian scholar, and I think very good.

EH   Are the poems translated in meters?

MH   Yes. It's a little haphazard, perhaps—not systematic: some are, some aren't. But some come spectacularly close, particularly Brodsky's best-known poem in the English-speaking world, the "Ode to John Donne," and I think Kline . . .

EH   . . . comes closest. You mentioned Auden's coming closest of all four translators.

MH   Yes, I think that's so. It's very hard to be definite about that. I think both Wilbur and Auden were very close to the original, but of course that's not to say the others were very far from it. No, I find it difficult to say.

EH   I mean, you're the one who has the knowledge of the Russian and sort of sit there in the shadows. . . .

MH   I think in terms of fidelity to the original it would be very hard to say who was closest. That obviously depended to a large extent on me. There was never any question of their not accepting my word if I thought they had strayed too far in sense. When it comes to closeness to the spirit of the original, again it's hard to compare them. What I would say, however, is that to some extent what struck me was that they were all true to themselves. They sounded like themselves as well. Auden, particularly, I thought sounded very Auden.

EH   He couldn't escape sounding Auden.

MH   . . . couldn't escape sounding Auden.

EH   And Wilbur sounds . . .

MH   And Wilbur sounds Wilbur, yes.

EH   Still you feel that they both did—what? They were more faithful to the original than the others were?

MH   Yes, insofar as they could interpret the spirit of the original, you know, through me. I think they were all faithful to it. I should say, incidentally—this is a very important element in the exercise—that they only did things that were congenial to them. In all cases they were given a choice of literal versions and in all cases they selected things that they felt were close to themselves, to the sort of things they themselves did. This is very important. I mean some poems were violently rejected. You know, "I just couldn't do this, or wouldn't be interested in this at all."

EH   Your role must have been very important, though. That paragraph I showed you, from my conversation with Wilbur, indicated to me that you had a lot to do with his translations. And yet it would be hard to determine exactly what it was you had to do with them.

MH   My general procedure was first to offer each of the poets concerned—I was working with them simultaneously for the Voznesensky volume—a large selection of fairly literal versions, and they each decided what they would like to do. And then I would work with each of them, first by submitting the literal version, plus a transcription—the transliteration from the Russian—so that they could see (with accent marks added) what the prosody was. Some were more, others less interested in that. But in this they were all quite rightly very, very free. None tried to stick to the original pattern, but they liked to take account of it, of course. I think this is absolutely correct. I think one should not limit oneself to the original prosodic scheme. In fact it's fatal to do so, in most cases. And then when I would hand them the material, which was essentially three things. . . . Oh, possibly apart from an absolutely literal version with the transcription under it, word for word, so they could see which Russian word corresponded to which English word, there'd be a translation into fairly normal English, so that they could read it and make sense of it. I'd give them these three things, they would look at them, and then I would go ahead and discuss them.

EH   So you did all the preparatory work?

MH   Yes. Then I would answer their questions and explain all the background to the poem. It was very, very important, incidentally, that they knew about the poet and the poet's work in general. It's not enough, obviously, to take an isolated poem and see it as part of the poet's oeuvre.

EH   You were giving them a short course in the poet?

MH   Yes, a short course, exactly.

EH In both the poem and the poet?

MH Yes, and in the general situation. This is also terribly important, because often in the case of these modern Russian poets there was a good deal between the lines to be explained. It was very true of some of Voznesensky's poems on American themes. Sometimes there were implications—and I think one can say this now without prejudice. . . . some of the poems on American themes, like Yevtushenko's, do have a certain Aesopian or allegorical undertone, and this had to be understood but not brought out too much.

EH Yes. The attitude is different then, of course. What you're suggesting is that a Russian poet writes in an environment where he must be very careful what he says and how he says it. Then to be translated by an American who doesn't write in such an environment but is sympathetic and wants to bring out what is in the original, would make the job so difficult at times as to seem, as you say, impossible.

MH Yes. Well, they were of course fascinated by this aspect of the job. It was something they'd never faced themselves, you see, but were very sympathetic to. They understood the implications of what a poet may intend and always has to think about. A Soviet poet, of course, often has to worry about a poem being taken with implications which weren't intended.

EH Yes, and that would also be hard to avoid.

MH Very hard to avoid. Voznesensky was sometimes attacked by hostile critics for implying certain things in his poems. It's a terrible game.

EH It's the extreme of the normal situation in which poets of one school are looked down on by poets of another school who can easily find the flagrant material in their rivals' work to criticize.

MH Yes, but this of course applies to Russian writers in general. It does sharpen the wits and is, I think, an important element in the literature. This isn't something crudely political, although of course it has a political dimension. But the fact that writers are aware of sanctions that could be applied to them if they overstep certain limits does produce a tension in the work, which is part of its literary quality.

EH Yes, the special awareness of. . . .

MH Of the dangers, the hazards, the difficulties. The image I use for this, and always bear in mind in reading modern Russian authors, is that of the difference between watching a man walk on the ground and watching a man walk on a tightrope. Because Russian writers walk a tightrope, there is a certain quality in their work that is absent from that of writers who can say what they like when and where they like it. It's important to appreciate this. I think you do see it very much in the work of poets like Voznesensky and Yevtushenko.

EH What about the older modern poets—Mandelstam, who's only just begun to be translated, and Pasternak and Akhmatova, Blok, Mayakovsky? Do you feel more work needs to be done in order to get them into good English? Or have they been treated well?

MH I wouldn't say so. I think in a way perhaps less well than some of the younger ones because they've been fortunate in the sense that there was a tremendous interest in things Russian after Stalin's death, and a number of people were then able to deal with them in some fashion. But the older ones I think have not been as fortunate. There are recent translations of Blok, quite good ones, by Jon Stallworthy, in collaboration with an informant, Peter France. There's quite a large selection of Blok. Those I think are the best I've read. Of Akhmatova there are several recent collections, including the one Kunitz did with me as an informant. A couple of others have come out in England this year. As for Mayakovsky, well, there have been lots. . . . But he, I think, has not really been well translated into English by anybody—although two or three years ago I saw some very successful versions of Mayakovsky into Lowland Scots by a Scotch poet, whose name I can't remember. He's well known but writes in Lallans, as they call it. Lallans is very much better adapted than English because it has a great vigor. It's phonetically much stronger than standard English and conveys much better this vehemence, you see, of Mayakovsky, flinging things into your face.

EH Sounds as though it might have been Hugh MacDiarmid.

MH It could have been but it wasn't he.

EH He's done six or eight songs about Lenin.

MH Yes, but those were originals and not translations. But it's MacDiarmid's kind of language.

EH Have you done translations with Patricia Blake? I ask because I frankly don't know.

MH No, we've edited things.

EH   But she like you has worked as an informant to other translators.

MH   Yes, she has helped on the project with the poets.

EH   And what of Olga Carlisle's volume *Poets on Street Corners*? Have you looked at it?

MH   I have, but I don't have anything to say. I honestly don't remember very much of it. It was very uneven—terribly uneven. There were imitations by Lowell in it. It was an enormous collection. I think it was far too ambitious.

EH   It was in response to a kind of need, was it not?

MH   Yes, but it would be very hard to sum it up.

EH   Because there isn't a great deal that has actually been done, one wants to know when such books come out what real value they have. I wonder if you have something to say about other contemporary Russian poets who haven't come through to us. Some observers tell me that there are many good ones of the stature of those we've been discussing who have not been translated into English.

MH   There's a whole new generation of people now in their twenties and early thirties whom I really know nothing about. But of those in their forties and fifties, say, of course there are very many. There was an anthology that Patricia Blake and I edited which contained some of the contemporary poets slightly older than Voznesensky and Yevtushenko. Vinacour was one—quite a good poet. Auden translated one of his poems. Who else? Bella Akhmadulina, who was Yevtushenko's first wife, and a first-rate poet, particularly in her longer poems. There's an extraordinary one on her family history called "My Genealogy," which is a title borrowed from Pushkin, about her great-grandfather who came to Russia as an Italian organ-grinder. A very good poem. And another called "The Rain." And she is, I think, one of the best, yet not much of her has been translated into English. Again there's a problem here with the long poem. It's difficult to do. Her best work consists of these long poems, and they're very difficult to sustain in translation. One can cope with a selection of lyrics to give some idea of the poet, but a long one is very hard.

EH   It's hard to make determinations about such matters, I know, but one interest of translation is that a new spirit is thereby brought into the language. And so I wonder if this may be happening with certain American poetry being picked up by Middle Europeans—say the Czech poet

Holub and the Yugoslav Popa, maybe even the Israeli Amichai—who respond to the snap and openness of William Carlos Williams, say. I wonder too if Russian could exert a similar influence.

MH I don't really know enough about contemporary poetry in America and England to judge, but I don't see any obvious influence. I wonder whether we're very open to influences now. It seems to me that there's such a basic state of confusion and ferment; I mean, our problem really is this openness and variety, which makes it very hard for an outside influence to find a focus. I may be wrong about this, but it seems to me that you can only have a strong literary influence from another culture when your own has been terribly isolated for one reason or another and therefore needs, desperately needs, this influence from outside as a reinvigorating element. And the West is simply not in this situation.

EH It's not in a situation to receive.

MH Yes, and I should think that the main importance of translating the Russians and others at the moment is really a natural inclination. I mean there is curiosity, there is a need to know—particularly in the case of a culture that has been isolated and hence thought to be rather mysterious. There's a great interest building in things Russian because of recent history. And while this is a little factitious, a little fortuitous, I don't think that it amounts to the exercise of an influence from that quarter.

EH What you say sounds true, but the impression that an excellent translation by a first-rate poet would make would most likely be transformative.

MH Yes, it might be. After all, it's probably a truism to say that a poet should not be influenced in any significant way. I mean, one should seek one's own manner; one should have one's own manner and style. One may be imitative, perhaps subject to influences at an early stage in one's work—the sign of one's formative period as a poet. But what a poet might want from other cultures would be inclination, as it were. You might want new myths, new images. But it's hard to see this kind of thing coming from Eastern European cultures to the West. Obviously no Western poet is going to be influenced by the manner of Brodsky, say.

EH Well, he seems to be a conservative poet.

MH Or of Akhmatova, to take some of the older ones, or of Blok. I think there can only be a question here of interest and curiosity, not of influence.

EH   There begin to seem ways in which Far Eastern poetry could affect the West.

MH   Well, this has already happened but is, I think, a very different thing. Obviously there is an enormous influence of the Japanese and Chinese forms, and this goes back to early in the century. This happened in Russia, too. There's a very slight Chinese influence, oddly enough, on Akhmatova, her early poetry. Perhaps it filtered through the West, through art nouveau and the rest of it. But later, very much later in her life, Akhmatova translated, it so happens, from Korean. There was some obvious affinity. It reminded her of her early work and took her back to that phase. The Far Eastern thing has obviously been an influence, but this is a totally different culture. It has therefore provided images and mannerisms. But you know all the basic forms of Russian and East European poetry are ultimately derived from the West, anyway. One would find nothing terribly new in them.

EH   We're talking about influence. I'm not sure now whether it's so much a matter of influence as of answering, as you would say, a need that a closed society has for a breath of air.

MH   Yes, there it's very important. Otherwise, certainly Russian has been enormously influenced by the West. Here one sees actual concrete influence. The influence of Hemingway on younger Russian prose writers is very distinct and evolved. There's no question about this.

EH   Hemingway more than Faulkner, for example?

MH   I don't think Faulkner has influenced them.

EH   He's harder to get through.

MH   Harder to get through, but Hemingway was something of a discovery, a very clear influence.

EH   Yes. Well, I suppose that influence is part of the business of translation, part of the parodic element in language that continually gets transformed.

MH   But the importance of translation probably is the very general one of broadening the horizon a little, and this leads to some enrichment— not to impoverishment anyway. Obviously, there have been times of extraordinary migration of whole styles between different parts of Europe, from East to West and West to East. But I don't think one should now expect anything like new trends or streams of movements to come across.

8 / Edmund Keeley

EH   Looking at your books of translation recently—I mean, the Seferis and Cavafy—I get the feeling that they were formidable labors. Would you tell me what motivated you to do translations initially?

EK   Originally, my motivation was purely practical. I was at Oxford in 1950 doing graduate work, presumably on Yeats's plays and the Irish theater. At the same time, I was trying to find somebody interested in modern Greek. I had just come from a year on a Fulbright in Salonika, and I wanted to make sure that what Greek I had relearned after a long hiatus would not be lost. I had first learned the language in Greece as a child, before the Second World War when my father was serving as American Consul in Salonika. After eight years in the States, having completely forgotten my Greek, I went back in the summer of 1947 and then again on a Fulbright in 1949–50. I wanted to make sure that I didn't suffer a further loss of contact with the language.

At Oxford I went looking for the Modern Greek Department, which, at that time, under Constantine Trypanis, happened to be one of the few in the world devoted to the subject. Trypanis convinced me to do a dissertation under his supervision on two important contemporary Greek poets. I knew nothing about them. I decided that might be worth looking into and found after reading Seferis, in particular, a contemporary tradition very close to T. S. Eliot. Since I had done a lot of work on Eliot at Princeton, Seferis seemed very accessible. He had also been translated well by Bernard Spenser, Lawrence Durrell, and Nanos Valaoritis,[17] so this struck me as an obvious area to explore. As I got into it I found that the existing translations were inadequate both in terms of the coverage

I'd need for any sort of serious dissertation and in the quality of the rendering. My supervisor at that time, Neville Coghill, told me that one way I ought to test my possible interest in switching from a dissertation on Yeats to one on modern Greek poetry would be to start translating the Greek texts. I translated a sample of nineteenth- and twentieth-century poets, and they were god-awful translations.

EH   Had you been interested at the time in writing yourself?

EK   I'd written some very bad poetry for what I hoped would be a creative writing course at Princeton under Richard Blackmur, but I was too late in getting to him. It became clear that I wasn't really going to be a poet, but I did think that I might become a playwright or a writer of short stories.

EH   Then it must have been a discovery for you—translation as a serious literary activity.

EK   Yes, but I didn't take it that seriously at the start. Translation originally was a practical necessity. I had to translate in order to have texts to serve for my critical discussion of modern Greek poets. Also, I think that around 1950 translation wasn't highly regarded by many. Neville Coghill was perhaps an exception. When he sent me home to do those exercises, he was thinking of translation as a creative act, and that's what interested him.

EH   Tell me a bit about Coghill.

EK   Well, he was the man who translated Chaucer into modern English, among other things, and he was a don in English at Oxford. Translation to him was a serious business. When he looked at my translations, he was judging them as poetry. It rather startled me when he'd say, "Can't you do this and that with the lines?" I'd reply, "Well, you know, I'm not at all interested—all I want is to get a kind of literal version." And he'd say, "There's no such thing." I didn't have time then to exploit what he taught me, because I was in a hurry to get the dissertation done and to get out of Oxford so that I could begin writing novels.

EH   This was an advanced degree?

EK   Yes, a D.Phil., which is the Oxford Ph.D. It was the first time a doctoral candidate had come to the Modern Greek Department. That's one reason why Trypanis was interested. Also, he himself was interested in modern poetry. Soon after I finished this dissertation, he started writing poetry in English, and developed a certain reputation as a poet writing in English, although Greek is his native language.

EH   Do you suppose you had anything to do with this development?

EK   Oh, I guess so—in a way. Not with his creative impulse; but in working with me on this dissertation he discovered Yeats, Eliot, and Pound, poets he'd barely known before that.

EH   So that became a source of excitement for him—through you.

EK   I think so. And the poetry he wrote, in its early stages, was strongly influenced by Cavafy and Seferis—the two poets I ended up focusing on in my dissertation.

EH   At what point did you begin to think of translation as a creative occupation?

EK   Several years after the dissertation was submitted. I included, as an appendix to the dissertation, a fairly large sample of Seferis's work in my English versions, that is, including poems that had never been translated by anybody, because the extant English translation, *The King of Asine and Other Poems*, was a limited selection—none of the early stuff, none of the stuff before *Mythistorima*. I included my versions as an appendix in order to give my dissertation readers some early texts to work with, one of the readers being Maurice Bowra, who didn't know modern Greek that well.

The case of Cavafy was easier, in a way, because there was a full English translation of his work by John Mavrogordato. It became merely a question of revising Mavrogordato, particularly those translations that were rhymed, where the sense was totally distorted. So the Cavafy texts I offered were a retranslation of already existing translations. I had no pretensions at all about my versions.

About 1954 I got the idea of doing a collection of modern Greek poets, and I was moved to do this to some degree by reading what I thought were very good new versions of Cavafy by Philip Sherrard published in *Encounter* roughly at this time—1955, 1956. I thought if I could take the Seferis translations that I had done and rework them and combine these with poems by Cavafy that Sherrard had translated, along with others which he had not done but which I had included in my dissertation, we then might be able to produce some sort of collection to fill the lacunae there.

Also, I had started doing some translations of Elytis one summer.

I wrote Sherrard to find out what else he had translated. He offered Sikelianos and more Seferis, also a lot of Elytis. He was with his family on the island of Thassos then, and I went up to meet him there in the summer of 1956, for the first time. I knew that he was the only other person around who had presented a dissertation in modern Greek, this at London University about the same time I presented mine at Oxford. I think it was in 1956 that he published his revised dissertation, which came out as *The Marble Threshing Floor: Essays in Six Modern Greek Poets* [London, 1956]. Sherrard was six or seven years older than I was and had already published a volume of poems.

EH I see. The coincidence was crucial. He seems precisely the right person to have looked up at the time. There was no one else translating modern Greek poetry then?

EK There was Kimon Friar; he had been working on the Greek poets for several years as well and had published some translations. I had met him at some point and had shown him my dissertation. He rather denigrated the translations. He said, "Of course these are not poems," and I said, "Well, they are not intended to be; they are part of a dissertation." But his comment again roused my impulse to make the translations come alive as works of art.

EH Was this the point, then, when you decided that the translations should be independent poems rather than aids to the essays?

EK That's right. They would be poems in their own right. But I'm still not sure that I thought of them as a purely creative enterprise. I had intended to abstract some material from my dissertation for articles, and in fact had done that essay on Eliot's influence on Seferis;[18] but, under the constant pressure to get things into print, I began to see these translations as new possibilities. I think I sent some revised versions to *Partisan Review*, and they were accepted. They took "The King of Asine," I think. Immediately translation became an important exercise, important in ways I hadn't conceived of at the start. So the fact that I had begun to publish a few translations in periodicals also gave a boost to my creative impulses in this genre.

And Sherrard proved to be not only terribly receptive to the proposed collection but very friendly in person. We became good friends quickly, and we've gone on being friends, over twenty-five years now. The dialogue we had on Thassos convinced both of us that there was a need for literary translations in our neglected field. There was no respectable anthology of Greek poetry. Cavafy had earned a certain amount of recognition, through Forster and Durrell, and Seferis a bit too, but only in England. Mavrogordato's version of Cavafy was published here in 1952[19] and got virtually no response. It was Lawrence Durrell's including Cavafy in the *Alexandria Quartet* at the end of the decade that really put the poet on the map. Seferis's *The King of Asine and Other Poems* was never published in this country. So there was an incentive to present generally unknown poets we thought were important.

What we did originally was really to stay out of each other's territory to some degree, dividing up the poets. Sherrard was to have Cavafy and Sikelianos, because he had done some Sikelianos already. I was to take the other poets; we hadn't decided exactly whom to include besides Elytis and Seferis. Originally I think we had those four poets in mind. Then I discovered Gatos and became very fond of him, both personally and as a writer, and I decided to do his small volume called *Amorgós*. And out of experimenting with a few others, we ended up with my doing the large part of two. Both of his major, one of mine major, and the others less so at the time. So it was really an even job.

I offered my translations, which he commented on only perfunctorily, and the same applied to my comments on his work. We put this collection together and shared the preface. Again, he did his half of the preface, I did my half. No real effort at fusion: anybody who knows his style and mine probably could decide very quickly which part of this preface is his and which is mine.

EH   Like twins, but not identical?

EK   Right. That was our first collaboration, and a strange kind of thing. It was a marriage of necessity, to some degree. When we came to do Seferis's *Collected Poems* about ten years later (*Six Poets of Modern Greece* came out in 1960 [London; New York, 1961], the collected Seferis in 1967),[20] there was more creativity and less necessity in the task. I think our incentive emerged after the Rex Warner selection of Seferis came out;[21] it was a pretty good version, but it left out many key poems. We thought we could improve upon both the selection and the translation.

EH   Having a collaborator must boost one's morale and urge one on. It's something a single translator might miss.

EK   Yes, the collaboration worked out marvelously. With the Seferis we did a different thing: we very arbitrarily divided the poems by going through the table of contents—this is yours, this is mine—not selecting on any basis of personal preference.

EH   I see—it's a bit like casting lots.

EK   With the slight exception that I got credit for the poems that I had already translated, and he for the Seferis translations that he had included in his critical study. The rest was divided up quite arbitrarily between the two of us. After we made up the list, we went our separate ways. I don't think we did any of these collaborative books while I was on leave, strangely enough. I was always doing something else that I thought of as my primary work, either writing novels or criticism or preparing new courses, and translating was the thing that I did for fun— though I assumed my work would be published and I therefore had to take it seriously. Translating satisfied the poet in me, too—the genre I'd abandoned professionally very early, but still loved and still taught. I always considered poetry the highest form of expression, that which I would aspire to could I . . . and so forth. Anyway, Sherrard and I would meet in Greece the following summer, and would have a preliminary chat about our progress to that point; but we usually waited until we could get together for an extended period, and then we would sit down and work very hard, reading our translations to each other, going over them side by side and reworking them quite thoroughly, so that by the end of the summer session it became very difficult to remember who had done which poems. The voice of the translation had somehow become a composite voice. A shared sense of what we were doing emerged from that. In the case of Seferis, the major problem was that of establishing density, of getting all the connotations we could into the text. This did involve questions of interpretation, to some degree; the language itself is not that complex on the surface, but it carries a dense richness of connotation.

EH   Can you give me an example of how you solved this problem?

EK   Well, the first that comes to mind is the one I discuss in that essay on problems in rendering modern Greek,[22] the substitution of *herald* for *messenger* in revising the opening line of *Mythistorima*. The revision attempted, not entirely successfully I'm afraid, to offer more than the standard classical connotation of the Greek *angelos*, the primary connotation that comes with the term *messenger*. Actually, *angelos* carries three connotations, just on the surface: the ordinary, everyday sense of "angel" (as in, "you're an angel"), the medieval sense of "messenger of God" or "heavenly angel," and the classical sense of the "messenger" who brings news on stage in ancient Greek dramas. I think the most important connotation of the three in Seferis's line is that of the angel who serves an annunciation, who introduces a new age of some kind of faith to replace the contemporary doubt and apathy. At the same time, he brings news that will help the poem's modern Ulysses and his weak companions "rediscover the first seed / so that the ancient drama [can] begin again." Sherrard and I (really at his suggestion) decided on *herald* rather than *messenger* (as all others, and we ourselves in our early versions, have rendered the word) because we wanted to emphasize that *Mythistorima* opens with this hope of an annunciation—obviously not fully realized during the course of the poem—for a new messenger of God who is brother to the messenger of the ancient gods and heroes, if now predominantly a heavenly angel (as in our "Hark the herald angels sing . . ."). I don't know whether *herald* really works better than *messenger*. The Greek is simply too rich for any single English term.

EH It seems very fortunate to me that an Englishman and an American could collaborate, because one assumes the English language is a different kettle to each. Also, I thought after reading what you wrote about the mixture of demotic and pure Greek being a special problem in translation that that too would further complicate things for your various renderings of the poets.

EK Well, we didn't just accept each other's English; we agreed on a neutral language, that is, a language that would not be so obviously British *or* American that it could be so identified. And when various quirks appeared, either of syntax or vocabulary—they were automatically resolved by a neutral term.

EH Well, it would come down to a matter of widest usage, wouldn't it?

EK Yes, a matter of usage. I think in this example in the case of Cavafy it became a question of idiom, "that's a lot of garbage," meaning "that's baloney," and I think we probably ended up settling for something less specific and local, like "that's a lot of nonsense," or whatever.

EH Were there many cases of this sort of thing?

EK There weren't many. And Sherrard was very good, you know. All I had to do was say, "No, that's British, we never say that in America," or "That's unnatural in American usage." I think by the time that we got to the final version of the Seferis the language of contemporary poetry had become Anglo-American.

EH   British English had begun to absorb Americanisms, even more rapidly than during the Second World War. And don't forget the Beatles, who quickened that tendency in the sixties.

EK   Yes, and somehow contemporary poetry had moved toward what we were aiming at, so that there was no need for great debate any longer.

EH   Well, let me shift to something analogous, concerning changes in style and idiomatic structures. In reading your Seferis this morning, I became aware at a certain point in the book that the idiom had changed. I mean, the level of diction had changed from that of informal to one of colloquial or even to slang usage. That made me wonder if there was something at work which you have discussed in your essays, in the stylistic versatility of Seferis's use of demotic Greek. I'm looking for this example now.

EK   I'm curious to know where you find it.

EH   I'm sorry I don't seem to be able to spot it immediately. We'll find it later. Well, there is also an aspect of the same question, I suspect, in translating Cavafy. Since I don't know Greek, one way I can talk about it is to tell you about a possibly similar experience I had in translating Fernando Pessoa, the modern Portuguese poet. Pessoa was very keen on Walt Whitman, and like Cavafy, Pessoa had a British background, having attended a South African high school. So he knew English perfectly well all his life. During his adolescence he apparently learned about Whitman too. Well, the point is that in translating Pessoa, particularly his long poem, "Salutation to Walt Whitman," I deliberately used a conversational idiom, a form of dramatic speech based on Whitman, because I felt this to be inherent in Pessoa's Portuguese. A Portuguese writer later told me that this was indeed so, that Pessoa's Portuguese was very unusual in this poem, being freely vernacular and even slangy. Now I wondered if the same thing might be true of Cavafy, since he too had a mixed linguistic and cultural background.

EK   With Cavafy it's not so much a matter of language level—that is, of the language level that he chose to maintain—as of the syntactical forms he used.[23] On the linguistic side, he is eccentric, but the eccentricity comes not so much from the fact that he was educated in England when

he was very young (roughly between nine and sixteen), but from the fact
that his Greek was learned partly from his mother, who had a Constantinopolitan background. You find Constantinopolitan forms in his poetry
much like the forms I encountered growing up in Macedonia, where
there were many refugees from Asia Minor. There are certain syntactical
quirks that are very characteristic of Greeks from Asia Minor, particularly from Constantinople. These crop up in Cavafy's poetry every now
and then, and their presence is quite surprising. Also, a certain linguistic
eccentricity in his work comes from the fact that he lived in Alexandria
all his life, and had very little connection with mainland Greece. These
two influences, I think, explain the eccentricity of his Greek; also his not
being afraid to use purist Greek (*katharevousa*) forms, which were really
very much on the way out in mainland poetry by the time he began to
write his best work—at least among the serious poets, like Palamas and
Kariotakis. But I think that what he did learn from his reading in English
literature, among other things, was the dramatic monologue form. I am
certain that he was strongly influenced by Browning, for example.
There's also an influence from the poets of the Greek anthology in this
area too. After all, they wrote monologues long before Browning did—
different kinds of monologues, admittedly. But I think that the sophistication Cavafy shows in handling the monologue form came from his
reading in Browning; and I'm sure there are certain English influences he
ultimately rejected: late nineteenth-century aestheticism, for example,
the Oscar Wilde mode, which fortunately went out of his poetry early
enough to allow his true voice to take a rather different direction, most
clearly in his work after he turned forty-five.

EH   To introduce another tack, related to these matters of style and
idiom: it strikes me that modern Greek poets may have special advan-
tages. What most other poets resist doing or else are very painstaking
(and painsgiving) about doing is to use heavy historical or classical
mythological allusions. But this practice would be easy for the Greeks
since the allusions are themselves built into their language, and the subjects would come naturally to hand as well. Also, I imagine, the Greek
poet would be fortified by a sense of local identity—one's home town
and its history—in a way that Americans are not, nor many English
poets after Hardy, for that matter.

EK   Yes, I may have said some of that in an article I wrote on Seferis.[24]
In using mythology, for instance, Seferis has a tremendous advantage

because he can focus on a contemporary landscape and find the Greek gods there in the very name of a place or a setting, as in "The King of Asine" or in the poems on Mycenae; and he can do it very naturally, simply by evoking a living landscape. The ghosts are still there; they're there in names, they're there in other ways that a poet sees, and we don't find this business—as in Eliot—of transferring to an alien landscape a different tradition.

But of course Cavafy had another problem—a problem that he turned into a virtue. That is, he obviously didn't feel, at least in his later years, a clear, direct link to the centers of Greek civilization—centers, I mean, in the philological, philosophical, and geographical sense. His Greece was the Greece of the diaspora, of the Hellenistic and post-Hellenistic world. He turned that into a virtue by creating what looks to those who are trained as classicists to be a very original world, and a very exciting new interpretation of Hellenism. Well, it's not so new, partly because it draws on other ancient sources, sources that are sort of the backwaters of the classical tradition. But these nonclassical sources were just as real, and they were a part of Greek history. And, I suppose, it was his discovery of this territory, of ancient Alexandria to begin with, that really made him a major poet. It gave him a voice, and it gave him a felt mythology to work with. I would also say that there are certain dangers involved in this: I think that, finally, both Seferis and Cavafy felt terribly burdened by that tradition; it became rather overwhelming, and I get the sense that both of them, in their late years, were trying to break out of it or move beyond it. In the case of Cavafy, the poet worked toward a more universal perspective; the Greek tradition and the historical process became, to some degree, the occasion for irony—an ironic attitude toward those who see the tradition strictly from a chauvinistic point of view. And in the case of Seferis, it was a matter of getting away from a specifically Greek context. The *Three Secret Poems* seems to me much more personal, much more turned in on itself, more elusive rather than allusive. This may all be the result of a poet's having too damned much tradition to work with, the authority of it hanging over him like a heavy threat. And I think that Ritsos may now be suffering from the same burden. He appears at times to be overwhelmed by a sense of history, so that its presence becomes too insistent and the motifs it inspires too repetitive. On the other hand, his keen historical sense is one of the things that makes him a "national" poet, a literary spokesman for his country, in the tradition of Palamas, Sikelianos, and Seferis.

EH I have two other points to raise: first, I'm not yet clear about the ways in which the demotic or the looser spoken forms of diction become poetry in Greek; also, I'd like to go further, if you wish, into the implications of a poet's having a strong sense of place and history—and how that might relate to setting up a heroic or antiheroic view in the poetry. Does the poet make a deliberate choice, and does his choice affect what happens to the verse when it seems very prosaic—as in Cavafy? Then, how does Cavafy, for instance, sustain the tension and meaning or sense of imminence, and what happens when you come to translate him?

EK On the matter of a heroic versus antiheroic point of view, I'm not sure what you have in mind in raising the question of choice, but Cavafy clearly chose to bring his gods and heroes down to earth in most instances, and one of his modes for doing so was through the use of colloquialisms or low-key demoticism or a "prosaic" tone, especially when these appear suddenly in a dramatic and linguistic context that leads the reader to expect a heroic or celebrative or formal tone. Cavafy's ironic view of the heroic is often established by just such a "deflation," by an abrupt contrast between expected formality or ceremony and down-to-earth demoticism or colloquialism. I think I try to illustrate this in the article I mentioned earlier, with reference to Cavafy's irony about Julian the Apostate, especially in the poem "On the Outskirts of Antioch," which concludes with an image of Julian "blowing up" in rage over the fire that destroyed his attempt to resurrect the worship of Apollo in a temple that had become sacred to the Christians of Antioch. The term Cavafy uses in this instance is *ekase* (literally, "he burst"), which is as contemporary and down-to-earth and "prosaic," if you will, as the ordinary conversation of today's unheroic mortals on the streets of Athens. But more generally, I think there is always a danger in translating Cavafy—a danger, in fact, of making him more rhetorical than he really is, because he seems to read flat, and there is that temptation to jazz him up a little bit. One doesn't want to be accused of being a flat translator. Well, the Greek in one sense is terribly flat: there's very little direct imagery, figures, tropes, that kind of thing. And in translation, you inevitably lose something that takes the place of figures, which is his sometimes playful and sometimes eccentric use of the Greek language, or the mixture of high Greek and low Greek in curious, often effective ways.

EH You can't find equivalents?

EK You can't find equivalents that don't seem to create more problems than they solve. People have tried. Kimon Friar thinks that you ought to use Latinate forms to create an equivalent for Cavafy's purist forms. I think what you end up with in that case is merely stilted, outmoded Latinate English. Mavrogordato got a donnish tone that I feel overly localizes what Cavafy was doing. So you do have the problem of losing some of the poet's linguistic texture, and of seeming to render him too flatly, prosaically, but I think that's a chance you have to take; the less artificial strikes me as the more honest and effective mode. You find the right stance, maybe, by remembering that Cavafy was a very dramatic poet, and that the forms he chose were almost inevitably dramatic; whether they're dramatic monologues, or indirect monologues that use a strong persona, they always somehow offer speaking voices, voices that allow the translator to introduce a colloquial richness, I think, that doesn't cheat on either the poet or the tradition of living poetry in English, and that can be found at least to some degree in the original. That's what Sherrard and I finally decided: that we were not only going to bring Cavafy up to date in the sense of making his idiom close to the idiom of our best contemporary poets, but also that we were going to create a dramatic reality—that is, to have voices speaking the way human beings do, at least within the current conventions of dramatic poetry.

EH   That answers it for me in some ways, because the variety of speakers, or the implied persona taking the speaker's role, does induce another interest, which overcomes the loss felt at the absence of imagery in the poems.

EK   That's right.

EH   The poet translators I've spoken with say that equivalence and transformation are the main principles to go by. What you say Kimon Friar suggested is what many of them would resort to. But you suggest yourself that it mightn't be the best way.

EK   Well, it seems to me that your translation can't be really equivalent if it introduces into your English text something that has become alien to the language of poetry in your own language.

EH   So there are two things. One is veracity, or being faithful to the spirit, at least, of the original. And the other is how it sounds. And here, to mend the style too much makes for a violation of the original poet's style. Put another way: making something that is originally done in a natural way become odd and gnarled (while attempting too hard to make it "poetic") invariably brings about a violation of the original poet's intention. Hence it becomes a mistranslation.

EK   Yes, I think so. Some people say, "Well, Cavafy *is* strange too in the original." Yes, but he's not *that* strange, and he's using peculiarities that exist even with the spoken idiom. I mean, there *are* people who speak *katharevousa* (purist) for particular effect, if they're trying to be "official" or professional, or if they're just pompous. Few knowingly use Latinate English in our day for any natural purpose.

EH   Excuse me. I've found that reference now. What I was referring to awhile back was that on page forty-one of the Seferis translation, I became aware of a shift in rhythms. We can look it up now. It's in your bilingual edition. Here it is, the poem with the lines, "On the track, on the track again, on the track / how many times around, how many bloody laps, how many black rows." There's the incremental repetition: "the people who watch me, who watched me when, in the chariot, / I raised my hand glorious and they roared triumphantly." You probably had a very good reason for making one conscious of the rhythms. Were you aiming at something different here, or what?

EK   No, that is almost a word-for-word rendering. In terms of the repetition certainly. You've got *sti sfendoni* three times there, and you've got three phrases introduced by forms of *poso* coming after it. Then there are the two tenses of *koitazo* (watch).

EH   Well, but it does happen suddenly. That is, in reading the poem to myself, I suddenly became aware of a much stronger rhythmical element than had been there before.

EK   I think that says something about Seferis's development during the course of this long, twenty-four part poem. I happen to be very fond of this particular passage; I think it is one of the great moments in the *Mythistorima*, if not the greatest. There's more honest rhetoric in this section, emphasized by the repetitions, than I think you find in any other part of the poem. And I would guess that it was influenced by rhythmical modes that Seferis discerned in Eliot.

EH   Eliot's method or certain poems? Which ones?

EK   "Ash Wednesday"—no, not so much that as "The Hollow Men," if you focus on the repetitions there. And part of "The Waste Land": "Speak to me. Why do you never speak? Speak." That sort of thing. There are several instances where he half-imitates this particular rhythm. But when I speak of rhetoric here, it's a different kind from what we find in poems previous to this one, where there was a certain lyrical rhetoric, if you will, as in "sleep wrapped you in green leaves like a tree": rather lush, closer in its imagery to the pre-*Mythistorima* Seferis, the Seferis who was under the strong influence of French symbolism. . . .

EH   Sort of Parnassian?

EK   That's right, a little bit of that going on there. In the "track" passage there's a more dramatic rhythm, and this is what he says he learned from Eliot: a dramatic mode of expression. It's partly a matter of this exclamatory, repetitive mode and partly a matter of seeing things through characters: there is a persona talking in this passage, a modern Orestes. It's not quite the same voice that you find in his earlier poetry, or even in earlier sections of *Mythistorima*.

EH   That would explain why, perhaps, it suddenly popped out at me.

EK   Yes, I think so. It's a voice under pressure. This is a modern exile tormented by the ancient Furies, who have become bored and unresponsive. That's the game Seferis is playing. But the passage has Aeschylus behind it. And to some degree, Aeschylus's rhetorical stance, as much as Eliot's anyway.

EH   Can you say anything about the difference between the two poets you translated, and if Cavafy influenced Seferis?

EK   Well, certainly in terms of preoccupation, Seferis was very aware of Cavafy, and Cavafy was, I suppose, the strongest influence on Seferis. Now, exactly how he influenced him would take a lot of thought and definition, but Cavafy was the poet who haunted Seferis. Seferis was going to write a full-length critical study of him; he's written some very good stuff on Cavafy, probably the best that has ever been written, but it's mostly in the form of notes on individual poems. At one point he sat down to write a book on Cavafy and finally had to abandon it. The reasons are rather deep and no doubt very interesting. But I think what he said was, "I found Cavafy was no longer useful to me," either because he was too much of a burden or because Seferis finally wanted to move on in a different direction. But at one stage, Cavafy was very useful to him, that is, in helping Seferis to develop the sparse voice that dominates his work.

EH   And did you sense that feeling when you translated Cavafy and Seferis?

EK No, because I didn't know enough about Cavafy at the time. Seferis was the poet that I really fell in love with initially. When I first took up the two poets I wasn't old enough or, I guess, sophisticated enough to understand how very good Cavafy was. I knew he was good, but his poetry didn't touch my heart. I came to love Cavafy rather later, came to respect his life's work more than Seferis's. I can say this now that George Seferis is dead, God rest his soul! I wouldn't have dared say it in his presence, although Seferis, I think, would probably admit it—that the master was Cavafy. He always thought of Cavafy as his master.

EH Could you say anything about the experience of knowing the poet you are translating? Seferis, for instance.

EK It's a strong inhibition—here again, having a collaborator was an advantage. I think I would have been overwhelmed by Seferis if I had tried to do the work alone. Rex Warner probably didn't feel that way because he was of Seferis's generation and they were very close friends, grew up in the same period, and Seferis helped Rex Warner very directly. I don't think that kind of relationship could have existed between Seferis and me, although we were very close in some ways: much more of a father-and-son thing than buddies-in-arms. Sherrard was also close to Seferis, but the relationship between the two was slightly different because Sherrard was older than me, and I think we benefited from that fact. Seferis was not as ready, perhaps, to challenge the translation (he was dubious about translations in general) as he might have been had I been the sole translator; he respected Sherrard's authority to some degree before I came on the scene, and the two of us created a common front as his translators. Sherrard would also give me added courage in coping with Seferis's hovering image.

EH I was thinking of something of this sort before when I asked you how you worked in collaboration.

EK You know, when I would say, "My God, what would old George say about that?" Sherrard would add, "Never mind about old George, we'll handle old George. We'll go see him!" Because Seferis, although he claimed that he didn't know enough English to judge translations, was very possessive about his work and what happened to it in other languages. When I'd send him copies of periodicals having early versions of things we were ultimately going to publish in the collected Seferis, I'd get back postcards from Ankara or Beirut saying, "You got that word wrong!"—and he'd give a sometimes cryptic gloss on the word in question.

EH He would normally know what you were doing with his work?

EK Oh yes. It was always cleared with him.

EH So everything you translated you showed him?

EK Yes.

EH Then his attitude normally was watchful. Did he say you were doing a good job generally?

EK Yes, he was never negative about individual translations as a whole, and at the time we did the collected Seferis I don't remember that he had very much to say about it, either in general or specific terms; I mean, he had full opportunity to look at the manuscript in advance and to object to anything he chose to object to, but he apparently found very little to criticize. It was the early drafts of translations, during my green years, that brought on the terse postcards.

EH Do you think he had some principle, like "be as literal as possible" or "be as English as possible"?

EK Well, like most poets, I think he held the principle that the translator of his work should be as literal as possible. I don't know any living poet who likes the idea of the translator taking very much freedom with his sacred text. But Seferis protected himself in another way: by insisting that the Greek text be published *en face*. Then he would say, "That's my poetry; now what you're doing is maybe wonderful and beautiful and so on, but that's not my poetry—that's your translation," and he always kept the distinction between the two clear in his own mind.

EH Oh, but there *are* some poets who when they are translated have the opposite feeling, or at least openly state it in this way: "My poem exists in my own language. What you, the poet-translator, do, is another poem, so do the best you can and please try and write a good one. Don't let me be the cause of a bad translation. Worst of all, don't let me shackle you so you end up doing a slavishly literal thing."

EK That's a very generous and a very sophisticated attitude. I doubt that Seferis felt quite that way. I think that, without being obtrusive about it, or making his presence overtly felt, he liked to review what we were doing, and I feel he appreciated the fact that our translation ended up very close to the Greek in rhythm and texture, at least to the extent he could judge.

EH   Your translations, both the Cavafy and the Seferis, often come through as poems more than some of the others I have read.

EK   That sort of thing he would never judge, you see. On that level he would draw a blank. It was the question of getting at least the literal part right that concerned him. On the question of whether it was poetry in English or not, he said he had no capacity to judge. In a way, he was right—anyway, honest—about that. He said, in effect, "That's up to you as translators to judge and your tradition to judge."

EH   There is much difference of opinion in this area, too, of course, not about the method but about the result—whether what ensues is actually a poem or whether it's a faithful rendering, say, or whether it's neither one nor the other. It's a tough business to resolve, unless you can fathom the translator's intention. But often the intention is so obviously limited and constrained there's no problem.

EK   Well, that's partly what I meant when I said that there is an inhibition in translating a living poet, because it seems to direct your intention toward a less flamboyant, free, liberated rendering. At least this was so in our case. It did not occur to us to do anything that would approach an imitation. Maybe Sherrard and I don't really believe in doing imitations on principle, or maybe we feel that isn't the best use of our talent, but I certainly would not have attempted imitations in the case of Seferis. I think we were more liberated when we came to Cavafy. Certainly the difference between our early versions and either of our latest versions is, I think, pretty extreme.

EH   The example you gave in your paper was very convincing.[25] How about further work? Are you planning to do more translations?

EK   Yes, alas, a selected Sikelianos—perhaps the most difficult translating we've attempted. And I'm going to do some Yannis Ritsos on my own.

EH   May luck and sparks of genius continue to shower your efforts, joint and individual!

Eusebio Rojas Guzmán

9 / Octavio Paz

EH   As I was saying to you, Octavio, a moment ago, I feel a certain constraint to limit this discussion so as not to repeat matters you have already explained in print, except when they are interestingly problematical. So, first of all let me say that you, of all people I have spoken to, seem to know almost by feel, by intuition, that translation is an activity that in its purposes lies at the root of all art, together with all that a civilized and a savage man might strive to express. To begin, I'd like to ask about your own first experience as a translator. How did you decide that you must be a translator?

OP   I didn't decide really. It was—well, as always—an accident. But also, as always when we talk about accidents, we also talk about desire. When I came to the United States the first time, I said, "Well, I must learn English better, because I want to read American and English poets." So I learned English mainly to read poetry. Then, reading English and French poems, I felt that they should be known in Spanish. You see: it was desire, love—and with love, the desire for participation.

EH   When you became interested in translation had the chief English and American poets been translated—like Eliot and Pound?

OP   Eliot, yes, but not Pound. Until recently he was not very well known in Spanish-speaking countries. Eliot was widely and sometimes very well translated. I remember one of my first encounters with modern poetry. I was studying for my college preparatory examinations, and at that time, around 1931, there was in Mexico a good literary magazine, *Contemporáneos*. It was published by a group of older poets. In one issue,

153

featuring modern poetry, there were poems by Neruda, Borges, Alberti, Guillén, all of them not very well known in those years. I was struck by two translations: *The Waste Land* and *Anabase*. Eliot and Perse, both in the same issue!

EH   When you started to translate from another language, did you have a feeling during part of your working that you wanted to be the poet you were translating?

OP   Well, no, I don't think so.

EH   Your own experience as a translator extends over a number of years. You still translate?

OP   Well, sometimes, yes. When I like some poems. Or when I have been asked, or because I am a friend of the poet's. Many reasons, no? One of the main reasons for translating is a moral urge, a didactic impulse. I think that Pound translated many things—Chinese poetry, for instance, *The Confucian Anthology*—for didactic purposes.

EH   Yes, it was part of what he called the *paideuma*—the course of reading that every civilized English reader would need to follow (as this is presented, for instance, in *The ABC of Reading*), something he thought a lot about. I have read and recently reread your essay on translation in *TLS* a few years ago and want to ask about the two or three main subjects you bring up in it. If I understood you well, I naturally wouldn't be asking these questions, which derive from adding some speculative interests of my own. You speak of the texts as the subject of translation. And I have thought of the text as often being a variable quantity and quality. The famous phrase of Robert Frost's—"Poetry is what gets lost in translation"—doesn't cover the situation. If something is lost, something is also recovered. The feeling of what gets recovered or found isn't mentioned much. I mean, what Frost says is what has always been said, proverbially: translation is either impossible or it's a fraud. But considering the text itself—I think it's precisely the text that gets lost in translation, in a physical sense, because it has to be transformed. So I ask: is there anything that is stable in terms of the text?

OP   I should say that poetry is what gets transformed. After all, poetry is not merely the text. The text produces the poem: a set of sensations and meanings. Now, what is the text? The text is signs—these signs can be written or oral, and they produce meanings. Signs are material things, you can see or hear them. But you don't see meanings and neither can you touch them. Signs are things that produce meanings but meanings are not things. In prose the function of the signs is, mainly, to produce meanings; in poetry, the material properties of the signs, especially the sound, are also essential. In poetry you cannot separate the sign from the meaning. Poetry is the marriage of the sensual or physical half of language with its ideal or mental half. Poetry is "impossible" to translate because you have to reproduce the materiality of the signs, its physical properties. Here is where translation as an *art* begins: since you cannot use the same signs of the original, you must find equivalents. The text is lost but its effects can be reproduced through other signs; with different means, but playing a similar role, you can produce similar results. I say *similar*, not *identical*. Translation is an art of analogy, the art of finding correspondences. An art of shadows and echoes. What we have called transformation can be called analogy also. Translation is the art of producing, with different means, analogous effects. I think Valéry said something like that. Or, we can put it in a more radical way: translation is the art of producing, with a different text, a poem similar to the original. I will give you two examples of the transformation of the text. Pierre Leiris, the French translator of Eliot, *with his approbation*, rendered "In the room the women come and go / Talking of Michelangelo" as "Dans le salon les femmes vont et viennent / en parlant des maîtres de Sienne." He tried to reproduce the *effect* and he had to change the text. Translating a sonnet by Mallarmé—the famous sonnet nine—I had to face a most difficult line: "aboli bibelot d'inanité sonore." He is speaking of a seashell (a "*ptyx*") lying on a table or sideboard. I wanted to produce a similar effect by different means: "Espiral espirada de inanidad sonora." The idea of "bibelot" was slightly displaced, without disappearing, and I underlined that form of the seashell (*espiral*). But I preserved the idea of extinction (*aboli, espirada*) and the play of sounds (*bibelot, espiral*).

EH   Let's go back to the question of the text, or as I would prefer to put it regarding translation, "the absent text." (I don't know if I read the phrase somewhere or if I originated it in this regard.) At any rate, the idea of "the absent text"—the text that is not there—seems to point to a more useful way of thinking about what happens in translation. Of course it's true that a good deal of the poetry that we know about comes through the ear and not the eye. That is—aural/oral. And there's a tremendous renaissance of interest going on right now in oral poetry.

OP   You are right and I'm distressed when I *hear* the French critics speaking all the time about "writing"—*l'écriture*. I think that they are missing something very important. Poetry has always been *spoken*. Speech is something you hear, not something you read.

EH   So from the oral point of view, we see what otherwise has been latterly so hard to understand—as you put it, the false idea that literal translation is the only true or possible one.

OP   The literal is not a translation. Even in prose. Only mathematics and logic can be translated in a literal sense. Real prose—fiction, history—has rhythms and many physical properties like poetry. When we translate it, we accomplish the same as we do with poems: transformations, metaphors. . . .

EH   The term in Spanish for literal—what you call *servil*—suggests where the emphasis really belongs. Literal translation, if possible at all, does not make for an interesting literary effect.

OP   You know, perhaps we should say that there are three kinds of translation. One is literal translation, which is conceivable and useful in learning a language. Then you have the literary translation, where the original is changed in order to be more "faithful" and less "literal." And then you have another kind, imitation, which is neither literal nor faithful. The point of departure in imitation is the same as that of the literary translation: the original poem; its point of arrival is different: another poem.

EH   Each type is meant to serve a different purpose—a kind of special use—and to have a certain effect. My hope is to engage you more on the subject of "the absent text" as an avenue into the subject in its true depth. Because if it's true that most of the history of culture and literature involves poetry as an oral matter, without a written text (and of course there are still poets who hate to type a poem or write it down, and would much prefer to speak it), and if this is so, one sees that the creative act is a re-creative act at the same time that each "oral poet" (like the Homeric bard) is engaged in resaying the same poem in different ways.

OP   The creative act is made up of tradition and invention. To make a poem you have to have certain patterns like meter and, in many cases, rhymes also. Then, figures of speech. . . . All these are given, handed to you by your tradition. At the same time you must say something new, personal. So that when you write a poem you are inventing something, but you are also repeating something very old. When you invent too much, it's a disaster, because then you have a text that cannot be communicated. When you don't invent at all, it's a disaster, because then you have a text that is not interesting enough to communicate. It must be balanced. That same thing happens when you translate. Translation is only one degree of this balance between repetition and invention, tradition and creation. Perhaps we should say more: each original poem is the translation of the unknown or absent text.

EH   Good. Now there may be another way to put this, and it's what got me to thinking about absent texts. Somewhere I read (and it's documented in a recent book by George Steiner) that the Cabala states that in the beginning God's word was lost or broken up. That is, there existed an original, universal language as well as a word that summed up everything. From this point of view, it may be said that what the translation does and what the original tried to do are both attempts to rewrite, reform, and bring together some of the broken pieces of that letter. What I'm trying to say is: the attempt to recover a lost or absent text that once existed is at the basis of translation. But also: both the original and the translation are simply two attempts to do the same thing.

OP   You are right. . . . The idea that the world is a broken text is a variation—a frightful one—of the idea of the universe as a book. This image was popular in the Middle Ages and through the Renaissance. It was taken up by the romantics and the symbolists. Baudelaire says that poetry is essentially analogy. The idea of universal correspondence comes from the idea that language is a microcosmos, a double of the universe. Between the language of the universe and the universe of language, there is a bridge, a link: poetry. The poet, says Baudelaire, is the translator. The universal translator and the translator of the universe. This idea of poetry as translation is related to the Cabalistic idea . . .

EH   . . . as to the medieval idea of the world as the book of creatures.

OP   Everything was *signed* or put into signs in the sixteenth and seventeenth centuries. Everything could be reduced to an emblem—a signature. Dante at the end of the *Commedia* sees God, the Trinity, the mystery we can *see* but can't talk about—and he sees it as a kind of book . . . with loose, floating pages.

EH   Yes.

OP For the Greeks the idea of the word was central. Also for the Hebrews. In the case of our Hebrew-Christian civilization there is this idea of the Book.

EH Rouault says in *Sur l'art et sur la vie* that people, if you think of them in everything they do, are really collecting words and pasting them up somewhere. You see signs everywhere, you see books and papers. You see the hunger and the frantic pursuit of information as an almost universal activity. Almost everyone is engaged in putting letters on paper, in reading things, making out signs. And if you'd come to earth from another planet, you would say these people are crazed by the idea of letters.

OP I don't know if you have read *Logique du vivant* by the French geneticist Jacob. He explains that the whole genetic program of cells can be reduced to a single command: to duplicate. In order to achieve this self-replicating aim, they must die. In the program of the cells—I should say, the program of life—is written the word *death*. The key word of the message in all living organisms is death. Duplication and death. This message is spoken in thousands of ways and it is carried on by all creatures. That is universal translation.

EH Yes.

OP The universe speaks. And it says: die—and duplicate. All living forms are versions and translations of this phrase. Cells, stars, atoms, everything, are saying in a different language, the same thing. Here you see the universe as a book but as a book that has only one sentence and millions of translations of that single sentence. Not all are faithful—there are accidents, mutations, variants. And it has one exception: the human race. Because mankind refuses to die and doesn't want to duplicate.

EH Why do we refuse to die?

OP Each person feels unique, singular. Each believes that *he* is as no one else: an ego, a soul. The souls are the opposite of cells. They are unique and they don't duplicate. Man refuses death, the self-replicating program of the cells, and tries to save his unique soul in different ways, from work to art and from religion to science. He does not want self-duplication but preservation, or, if you like, self-perpetuation.

EH What do we want to preserve that is so important to life?

OP Cells want to duplicate because they don't have an ego; they are soulless. Man wants to save his soul or his ego, not his life. From the ego spring the two ideas that have obsessed us: that we are unique and that this uniqueness must be preserved in some way. This way is not duplication but transformation. Duplication is literal translation. Exact identity between the original and the copy. Transformation is poetic or literary translation. Man translates the universe and, by translating it, changes it. This applies to Baudelaire and the Cabala but also to science and culture. It applies to civilization. Think of the Chinese translating the Sanskrit texts, or the Jews translating in Alexandria the Greek Testament and the Romans translating the Greeks. The history of the different civilizations is the history of their translations. Each civilization, as each soul, is different, unique. Translation is our way to face this otherness of the universe and history.

EH Is it known about the Aztecs or the Incas, whether they translated?

OP They translated: they took things from other civilizations and what they took they changed. If you think that translation is not only a verbal phenomenon, then you can accept history as translation. In this sense, they did translate. And also in the verbal sense: pre-Columbia Mexico was a polyglot society. The Conquest can be seen as an extraordinary exercise in translation. As you know, Cortez had as interpreter a famous and intelligent Indian woman, who became his mistress: Malinche or Doña Marina. She knew Nahuatl and Maya, and at the beginning of her relation with Cortez they had to use another interpreter, the Spaniard Aguilar, a former prisoner of the Mayans, who knew this language and Spanish. From Nahuatl (Malinche) to Maya (Aguilar) to Spanish (Cortez).

EH An amazing set-up, presenting itself at a time when it was most needed. Now, I wonder if there's such a thing as a single source or original civilization. We speak, for example, of an Indo-European language, assuming an original though quite hypothetical language of that description.

OP You mean that there may have been one original language? I don't know, and even if it could have been, I don't think knowledge of the fact would have an important bearing for our purpose. I believe that there always has been, from the beginning, a plurality of texts. You were talking about the absent text—the "idea" or archetype of the text. In reality there is not a single text; there is always an *Ur*text—the never written and never spoken "original," always virtual and always appearing in many versions, all saying the same thing and saying different things. And that is the paradox of literature, I think, and of art: the great works say the same thing, and at the same time say it differently.

EH   You've said that now very well in the same way that I was reading it before in your essay, where you speak about the translation conjoining—through the limits of separation between languages—languages that are always changing. Actually, I had a question to ask you about that. When does any translation stay put? When does a translation stabilize itself? That is, one is aware of languages changing all the time, so that the language of the last generation is not our language. But there are certain works that persist, no matter how much the language changes. The King James Bible, or, if you regard Shakespeare as a good translator of Plutarch, which he is, *that* stays put.

OP   Well, Shakespeare is one moment of the text, a kind of pivotal figure of the processes to follow.

EH   Now, this is also related: certain translations continue to be fresh and marvelous, even in an antiquated form of the language. The vigorous sixteenth-century translation of the *Celestina*, for example, by Thomas Mabbe, the Englishman, is still a joy to read. Against the rule that there need to be new translations every generation, this is a rare phenomenon. Of course there is such a thing as a sacred book, as Homer in a sense once was, and as Shakespeare is now, a book sacred to our culture, you might say. In fact, what we regard as classics in art and literature are moments of sacred artistic accomplishments.

OP   And those books are the most widely translated. You know, I'd also like to talk about the practice as well as the theory of translation. We start with love. You *must* love the text. Then, you must know your own language and also you must have a good knowledge of the text you are translating. You must work very hard, have very good dictionaries, a good technique, and finally inspiration. Inspiration is something that comes not from the stars but from inside, from working. Inspiration is linked with work and is linked with the dictionary. Without the dictionary you don't have inspiration.

EH   A dictionary—that's another book!

OP   It's the book as the universe, again. It is the sentence, but the broken sentence. The dictionary is the real double of the universe—only it is broken, disjointed. With the dictionary you can make all the books, but which would be the Real One?

EH There's one other aspect to this, the relation between translation and creation. You experimented in such a way with the *renga*, the versions of poems in four languages by four different poets—a very interesting way of re-creating poetry. What it does is exactly to bring together the translation and the original in one act.

OP Yes, it's true. *That* is the thing: the transformation, the changed text, coming from a text in English, then one in French, one in Spanish, then Italian. All these transformations are a creative and not simply a mechanical process.

EH This interests me as a psychological use of game playing with language. In a way, it's a joke, but also a sort of controlled "experiment" of four different-language poets who pretend to be subjects of some kind of master idea, to which they are bound to respond. You explained it as taking place in a hotel basement in Paris overnight. Can you say something about the *renga* game?

OP You can also say it's an experiment in the sense that we were trying to be both the objects and the observers. It could also be called collective writing. And a ceremony or a game—all this together. A game, because it was subject to rules and was a gratuitous activity; a rite, because we were doing something very old: trying to reactualize a Japanese practice of a poetry commune. And then the idea behind that was that we were only the instruments of *another* author. This author was the language itself—the language that was also changing as we wrote, changing with the tongue of each poet. It could be summed up as a game, experiment, joke, rite, mystification, ceremony. When you are writing your own poem you are doing the same thing. It is a game and a ceremony—don't you think? A rite.

EH What did you feel about the poems that came out of it?

OP Well, I think I should not say anything about the poems. I'm one of the authors. . . .

EH I don't blame you.

OP I believe the primary thing was the activity. I was thinking of doing it again, but in only one language.

EH Well, that too would be interesting. There is, of course, a game of that sort that's well known. Someone creates the first line, and then mails it to someone else in another city who adds another line, and so on. It's a chain letter.

OP The surrealists played a similar game and it was called "the exquisite corpse."

EH Something both primitive and sophisticated.

OP Speaking of the *renga*, you know the surrealists were very addicted to spontaneity, the unconscious, and chance. And in this sense our *renga* was not surrealist. It was chance but controlled. It was accident but also according to rules. Only in a work done according to the rules can you have accidents..

EH But did you feel that while you were engaged in this collaborative poem, the rite and experimentation with the languages, that you were also repeating an experience that was natural and very old, going back to what is called primitive society?

OP The *renga* is not that ancient. It was done in the fourteenth century.

EH I was thinking of the activity of shamans.

OP Yes, there is a relationship. *Renga* is only one form of the old and universal practice of collective poetry. We can say that poetry is always collective because you always have a reader or a listener. Always, at least, two: the text, the voice—and that listener. But I have read that there's a tribe on the frontier of Bolivia and Paraguay. They're nomads. And these people, who are very few, hunt all day. They make camp at night, and, after the meal, the men go to face the night, on each of the four different parts of the horizon. And there they invent poems that they say to the spirits of the night. It is all about their prowess in hunting, a kind of epic poetry that the hunter makes for nobody but the night and its spirits. Is that not moving?

EH Yes, indeed.

OP It could be the negation of translation. That could be the great exception.

EH It's true.

OP When you're reading a poem, you're translating. When you're reading Shakespeare, you're doing a translation—translating him into the American sensibility in the twentieth century. But the poem of the hunter would never be heard and translated—it's all meant to be between him and the night only.

EH   Isn't that where it begins, between a man and some voice that calls him, and he has to answer? I remember when I was a boy reading the Old Testament in Hebrew and being very awed by. . . .

OP   You can read Hebrew?

EH   I did then. I can make it out now. When God said, "V'yomer Adonai el Moshë," "and God said to Moses, Come," and Moses said, "I am here, *Hineni*, I am here," I think of that connection as a sort of formula, presenting a very dramatic moment. When God called man and he said, "I am here," they established a conjunction. So that whatever was said, as God told him to do this and that, was said only between the two of them. Later, when Moses went up on the mountain and he was alone there, for however long he was there, it was a very terrible moment, because maybe it was like that moment you just described with the Indians in the night. The moment of being alone with the creator and one's creation.

OP   With your soul. When the hunter talks with the night and the spirits, he talks to himself. The reader, the listener is—yourself. Many times as a boy I used to hike in Mexico, when we had a beautiful valley, which isn't beautiful now, since it has become polluted. But then it was very beautiful to walk through, and sometimes you cried out and you heard the echo, and that's all. Our great solitude in nature.

EH   The last syllable of the word. You're talking about the last syllable—"the last syllable of recorded time."

John Bellby

10 / Michael Hamburger

EH   Well, Michael—I'm aware you're one of the best English translators of German poetry there is. You've been at it as long as I've been conscious of translation. Also, you've worked from languages other than German.

MH   I've done French and Italian, though my Italian is not very good. I have translated occasionally from other languages that I know even less than that, but it was only when I was writing a book for which I needed translations that I couldn't find, so I tried translating the things for myself. That was from Portuguese and Spanish.

EH   You've always translated for pleasure or gain, or both?

MH   Mainly for pleasure. I started translating when I didn't need to earn any money at all, at the age of sixteen or so, at school, and I've done it ever since. Certainly, at first there was no question of gain at all. Nor have I actually earned much money at it because I've always translated things I've wanted to do and not things I was asked to do.

EH   Did you feel that the texts you were interested in had not been done well before? Were they new?

MH   In most cases they had *not* been done, or if they had been done I wasn't aware of it. I started off with the German poet Hölderlin. Well, I had done some translations before that, of rather poor or mediocre poets whom I liked when I was a kid of fifteen or something. Once I discovered Hölderlin I got down to that quite seriously, and actually had a translation done by the time I was eighteen, which was published the following year. I regret that now, since it was inadequate. Though it apparently fulfilled some purpose, answered some need, because it was the first larger selection of Hölderlin's poems to appear in English, and through that collection many people got to know Hölderlin who never heard of him before.

EH   You said you were often unaware of the existence of other translations when you began. Is this true in each instance?

MH   In the case of Hölderlin I discovered later that there were a few, but actually there was no large book of his poems in translation. There've been a few done by David Gascoyne, but he had translated them from the French, actually, because he doesn't know German. These were only fragments that were of interest to the surrealists because they anticipated certain surrealistic things that had been done into French, and Gascoyne discovered them. Then, much later, I discovered that a very obscure American had done them—even earlier, I think.

EH   Was it Frederick Prokosch?

MH   No, Prokosch was doing his about the time I did mine, and in fact his came out, if I remember, a bit later than my first version, but there was a man—I think his name was Loving[26]—who worked in some rather remote part of America and was not known to anybody. I only discovered that later when I went into Hölderlin scholarship more. . . . I've never actually possessed the book, but I had the impression they weren't terribly good. They were done at a time when hardly anybody knew about Hölderlin.

EH   Hölderlin bears the same relation to German surrealism as Rimbaud and Lautréamont do to French.

MH   Yes, the surrealists were interested mainly in his very late work, written on the brink of madness, where there are very strange images that do look like surrealist writing, though, in fact, they're quite different, of course.

EH   Were you interested at the time in writing poetry yourself?

MH   Oh, yes. I started writing my own poems about the same time.

EH   How would you describe your knowledge of German then?

MH   I had my German really from birth, since I was born in Germany and spent my early childhood there. It was my mother language, but one that I partly lost again because I then grew up in England after the age of nine and for a long time I never spoke any German. Also my German was pretty rudimentary, because it was a child's German. Afterwards, I learnt it again; I did German at school, and then at Oxford.

EH So you sort of specialized in that language.

MH Yes, and in French. I did Modern Languages. I started specializing in German and French at school, before I went to university.

EH From your experience as a poet and as a translator of poetry would you say there is a difference between translating poetry and prose? Is it a matter of form—I mean does prose have a form that needs to be contended with in translation as poetry does?

MH If not a form, then a rhythm. I think certain kinds of prose are just as hard to translate as poetry. You have to observe rhythmic qualities just as much as in translating verse. In fact, my view is that a great deal of poetry is more translatable than some prose. I'm talking here of imaginative and not scientific prose, of course. I find this true, for example, with a lot of novels. If I read a novel in translation very often I have the feeling that whatever world is being captured in the novel simply does not come across in the translation at all because so much of the substance of the novel is in the original language and the way people speak it. Because people have different associations with different words and so on, the whole point of the novel might well be lost in a strictly literal translation. I think this rarely happens with poetry, except perhaps folk poetry or dialect poetry—or certain other varieties. It also happens with plays. Some plays lose enormously in translation when translated literally, for what then comes out in the other language is something completely different.

EH A matter of flavor?

MH Flavor, yes, the whole atmosphere of the work. For example, I edited a two-volume selection of Hofmannsthal's works, and I found that the poems, although written in a very peculiar kind of language, are more translatable than any of his plays. His prose plays, which are perfectly straightforward, are written in an idiom that I suppose you'd say is a distillation of the way the upper-class Viennese spoke, but it's not exactly how they really spoke because the language is intensified. It's perhaps something like what Synge did with the language of the Aran Islanders—which, again, is not how they actually spoke but a distillation of their way of speaking. Well, whatever is done with this sort of play, although it's set in the twentieth century, you cannot find any kind of idiom that corresponds to its particular language. To find anything resembling it you'd have to go back to seventeenth-century Restoration comedy. But if you do that, of course, you're creating a period piece and you're destroying the atmosphere of the original play.

EH You must have known a good deal about Viennese German to become aware of the special language in the Hofmannsthal play.

MH Oh, yes. I took some interest in that. I went to Austria. At that time I did quite a lot of work on Hofmannsthal, and in Vienna at that time I was looking for unpublished material which I later found in London where I lived.

EH Well, to return to the vexing question of translatability. One point of view is that nothing is translatable. This is what Willard Trask says, then adds, "Therefore I translate." The challenge is always there, a creative tension to overcome. Others say that some languages are more difficult or impossible to translate into English because they are so formally different. About German, I'm not sure; I haven't translated enough from it to know, only some Rilke. Is it all a matter of kindred languages being translatable and others not?

MH Well, I would say that on the whole German is more translatable into English than French. Here I'm not talking of prose because very classical, lucid French prose translates into English perfectly well. But French poetry, I would say, is hard to translate into English because it's so different in the way it works. It rarely succeeds. Racine, for example, has been translated fairly recently into English in a way that works quite well on the stage. But for centuries Racine was not really known in England and not actually played or acted on the stage because there were no translations.

EH Racine didn't lend himself to the English stage?

MH No. I think it's the same with lyrical poetry. I don't know precisely why French lyrical poetry is so hard to translate. I think it's partly because the versification is so rigid while English versification is incredibly flexible. If you look at almost any poems in English written in iambic pentameter, so called, you'll find that out of three lines only one is regular—and even that frequency is unusual. Sometimes you'll find that only one out of eight lines is regular pentameter. English poetry is full of variations, whereas French is very inflexible. This was true, of course, until the time of Laforgue and Rimbaud, who deliberately set out to break the laws. And that, I think, is one reason why the prose poem was cultivated in France in the nineteenth century while there was really no need for it in English because in blank verse there is great flexibility. But there was no blank verse in France, and this is one of the main differences between the two poetic traditions.

EH   Is there any connection between the inflexibility of French verse and the declamatory way in which Racine is enacted?

MH   Yes, I'm sure there is. It is related to the whole idea of rhetoric in poetry. I would say that French poetry, in fact Latin poetry altogether, is far more declamatory and rhetorical than English verse. In German some poets are translatable, some are not. The ones that tend toward folk song—and a lot of German poets do—are the hardest to translate. That's why some of Goethe's best lyrics have never been successfully translated—they were modeled on folk song.

EH   Some of these are in *Faust*?

MH   A few are in *Faust*. Several early lyrics, like the famous "Sah ein Knab' ein Röslein stehen," are in fact a kind of folk song; they have become folk songs and are sung by people in German as such. And they are very hard to translate.

EH   You seem to be forming a principle here: the closer one gets to a folk flavor in a language, the harder it is to translate into English.

MH   Yes, I would say that.

EH   Have you tried to get the folk flavor in your translation?

MH   I have tried, yes. Mind you, it could be approximated perhaps, for example in the Scottish Lallans. Lots of poets in Scotland have succeeded in doing some excellent translations into the Lallans dialect. It is both a folk idiom and almost an artificial language evolved for the purpose of making poetry, and so it had that folk quality to it. Certain things come off in Lallans that don't come off in neutral or general-educated English.

EH   You're thinking of poets like Hugh MacDiarmid. . . .

MH   Yes, he's done it. And then a lot of people after him—Tim Scott, Sidney Goodsir Smith—a lot of them.

EH   You feel these poets have extended the idiom—well, not of English itself, precisely; but because they can write in a dialect more kindred to the German, they're able to touch the real thing. Has any of these people tried to translate Goethe?

MH I don't know specifically. I remember Villon, for example, coming out very well in Lallans.

EH I recall that MacDiarmid was something of an experimental writer. A book of his called *In Memoriam James Joyce* is a long poem using dialects and various languages. . . .

MH Well, he has done some translations. I think he translated some things from the German too. If I'm not mistaken, he translated some Rilke.

EH That's an interesting sidelight—it's possible for a sophisticated poet using a dialect to reinvigorate the language, at least indirectly.

MH Well, yes. I think that the language most people in the twentieth century speak is particularly unpoetic and that's why there are many things that you can't translate into it. I think the more esoteric and hermetic the poetry, the easier it is to translate, while poetry which is close to folk song is not easy. That's really what I'm getting at.

EH Has translating modern German poetry influenced your own poetry?

MH That's a difficult question to answer. I'm pretty sure that it has, but I wouldn't be able to say in detail how. I think the only poet whose influence I'm aware of is Hölderlin because he's occupied a special place in my translating. I have, in fact, spent twenty-five years translating him. I did that early translation, but then I did another version, and then another, and then a fourth version.

EH You've published all these?

MH I've published four versions and they're all different. I added to them all the time, so that as I did more and more poems I kept revising the early versions. There are certain things in Hölderlin that I admire so much that I'm pretty sure they have in some way entered into my work. Not obvious things. For example, not his themes at all. Not the subjects he writes about, because they are quite remote from my concerns. It's a matter of articulation, really. He had a special way of articulating a long poem so as to produce a dynamic that sometimes overruns the stanzas, where the syntax is almost independent of the meaning. Often it's not the syntax of rational discourse at all. It's a syntax devised for purely poetic effect. Hölderlin builds up out of the sentences a kind of architecture, as he called it. For example, he will start a sentence and leave it suspended, and then start another inside the first. He does this deliberately because he wants to create a kind of suspense, which becomes the form of the poem.

EH Sounds very modern.

MH It is modern, in a way, but it's also very ancient. A lot of it derived from very ancient Greek poetry. And that's where he took a lot of his ideas too. So I think all of this has probably influenced me in my own work in some way.

EH You've written about Hölderlin too.

MH Yes, I have.

EH I'll spare you having to repeat what you've written elsewhere. But I would like to ask whether Hölderlin's devices compare at all with Gerard Manley Hopkins's use of language.

MH Hopkins is a very peculiar case. His antecedents were quite different from Hölderlin's. Hölderlin began with classical poetry—Greek and Latin, but mainly Greek. In fact, most of his work is written in adaptations of Greek meters, which are either the lyric meters, like the Alcaic ode, the Sapphic ode, the Asclepiadean ode, or elegiac meter. Then, lastly, Pindaric meter. In fact, he was one of the first German poets to understand classical meter. It's very strange, but in the eighteenth century, in German, people were writing free verse. The reason they were writing free verse is that they thought they were imitating Pindar. Pindar's odes look like free verse, if you don't understand how the meter works. The meter there doesn't carry through from stanza to stanza, but it carries through in the triads of stanzas because each triad constitutes one of three different voices. You have one voice, you have another voice, and then you have a chorus. There is actually a metrical correspondence between each voice, the different strophes given to each voice. Hölderlin was one of the first to imitate strictly the Pindaric ode in that way. Then he gave up trying because he realized that these odes originally served a definite public function; they were performed. Since this function no longer existed it was useless to imitate the forms. But out of this experience he developed a free-verse form which he used for some of his greatest poems, his late poems.

EH So, experimenting with meters did pay off. I recall from my meager ancient learning that Ben Jonson did a strict imitation of a Pindaric ode which is supposed to have been the first done successfully in English.

MH Yes, but afterwards, in the seventeenth century, there were lots of so-called Pindaric odes in English. Abraham Cowley wrote a lot of them. One difference between the English and the Germans is that the English poets always translated into rhymed verse and used the iambic foot. The Germans, when they imitated ancient meters, didn't use rhyme and also used other rhythms, not simply iambic, but all sorts—dactylic and so forth. In fact they tried to imitate, much more closely than the English did, the actual movement of Greek and Latin verse.

EH Why so? Is German closer or did they have better models to imitate?

MH It's partly due to a kind of pedantry which the Germans are always accused of. If they were going to imitate something, they were going to imitate it thoroughly. That was how it began. It also had to do with the character of the language; because German has inflections like the ancient languages, it therefore lends itself much more than English does, for example, to dactylic meters, hexameters, and things of that kind.

EH For me German is mainly prose, the language of German prose, rather than poetry. That is, I don't hear the meters in German. But it seems to me that the hold of iambic pentameter, or the tradition of it in English, is not as emphatic in German.

MH Oh yes. A good deal perhaps came through French and Italian; in the Renaissance they started using those meters. The natural meters in both English and German are, in fact, sprung rhythms like the ones Hopkins uses, found again and again in popular verse—in ballads, in nursery rhymes, where the accents or stresses are the thing that count, not the number of syllables at all. That's why I think that iambic meter is really rather a limited meter, if one uses it all the time, consistently. I think that's where Hopkins hit on something very important—in reviving stress-metered work.

EH Did you find yourself using the iambic foot less as a result?

MH Well, no. That came independently of my translating. I had translated for a long time when I was still writing mainly in iambic meter because that's more or less what I had been brought up in and had accepted. It was solely when I had a kind of crisis in my life—I simply couldn't write any more—that I suddenly realized I *could* write if I broke the tyranny of iambic meter and started writing in other meters and in free verse. That was a kind of liberation, but I didn't really do it by thinking about it; it was just something that happened.

EH You mentioned crisis—I don't mean to go into personal matters here. But Lowell and other poets have said that often when poets turn to translation it's because they aren't writing their own work. Is this the case with you?

MH Well, yes—to some extent it's so. I can never really translate intensely when I'm writing my own things. It tends to go in periods. I don't know whether through translating I actually lose some of my own poems; I just couldn't say whether this is so, but I know that when I feel a strong urge to write my own things, then I put translation aside. But it has worked out with me, as far as I know, rather well. I do it sort of alternately. Now I translate, now I write something of my own.

EH But you're as much involved in the work when you're translating as you are when you're writing.

MH Yes. But it's probably a slightly different kind of involvement because it's an involvement only as far as the formal matters of the language are concerned. It's the difference between playing music and composing music. You have all the pleasure of playing music when you're translating and you're using all the skills you have. Although you're involved, of course, in the themes—insofar as you are trying to get into them, you're trying to get into what the poet you're translating is trying to say and trying to do—but it's still not the same thing as actually writing something that is your own. At least to me it isn't. It is intense, but it's not the same. The two kinds of intensity are different.

EH Have you ever looked into the work of other poet-translators or playwright-translators? I'm thinking of Beckett now. When he writes, as he does, in two different languages and then translates his own work from one into the other, something happens; he seems to rewrite more than he translates.

MH I have noticed this. It happens particularly when the authors translate their own things, because then they take liberties that another translator ought not to take and that only the author has the right to do when translating. It's very interesting that these liberties do have to be taken when writers are translating one of their own works into another language. I think that what they're doing then is rewriting their works in a way. They're not actually translating them; they are rewriting them according to the laws and needs of the other language, which are different. There's a contemporary German poet, Hans Magnus Enzensberger, whom I used to translate. At some point Enzensberger decided that he would translate his own things into English since his English is pretty good and fluent. But then when I looked at his translations, I found that he had written completely new poems. That was interesting to me. I have actually tried to translate one or two of my poems into German. I was tempted to take the same liberty and actually write a different poem but I didn't, only because I was doing this for a book that consisted mainly of translations of my poems by other people. Since they had translated the poems fairly faithfully, I felt that my translations would stick out if I did them another way. Because the book was going to be printed bilingually, I tried to do them more literally than I'd otherwise have done.

EH Here's one question I've been wanting to ask because I feel there's a hidden principle of translation lurking in what you've been saying. You seem to have said or to have implied several times that the translator does not have the liberty to do something that the author can't do. Then you have a view of the restrictions or limitations of what is translatable.

MH Yes, this is a personal thing. I realize there are different ways of translating. There are the past ways, as when Dryden talks of metaphrase, paraphrase, and imitation. These are still applicable to the translation of poetry—that is, three distinct ways of translating poetry. One very completely literal, the other—I think he says "translation with latitude"—he calls paraphrase, and then imitation, which is completely free and doesn't have to follow the text at all. I personally have never wanted to translate in any but the middle way; paraphrase is my kind of translation and that is what I practice. I've never felt the need to write imitations. I don't know why that is.

EH Then you see these as very distinct categories or methods rather than overlapping tendencies in practice.

MH Well, there are elements of overlapping. When you are translating as faithfully as I try to translate you do take liberties. You take liberties instinctively because you realize that in order to translate one thing into another language you cannot just put that one thing into the most literal equivalent thing you find because that would create a completely wrong effect. What you're aiming at is a faithfulness to the spirit of the thing and not only to the words. Therefore there is an element of invention even in more faithful kinds of translation.

EH There may be another way of putting this, and I would like to know what you think of it. That is, that there are, in fact, very few translators who deliberately choose imitation—a means of writing a free version—simply because it's harder to do. It's not only harder but in some way foolhardier, unless you have a total sense of the original that you want to supersede.

MH I don't think it's a question of its being harder, really. It's a question of feeling the need to write original work that is based on something else. I don't feel that need, you see.

EH The reason I put it that way is that a lot of the criticism of translation by people who look at it as a linguistic exercise, or even a literary exercise, based on a linguistic transferral, is that the writer always "takes too many liberties" with the text, whereas in fact anyone writing a translation *must* take liberties or else give up.

MH To me it's not so much a question of liberties but of whether the translator is trying to impose himself on the text or whether he is trying to render the text. In order to render the text one may also take liberties, but there is a difference here between somebody who simply uses the text as a springboard for his own exercises and inventions and somebody who is thinking primarily in terms of the text he's translating. I would say that I belong to the second category. . . . Well, there are some very strange exercises—those that Ezra Pound began with in the "Homage to Sextus Propertius" and then what Louis Zukofsky has done with Catullus, where he translates the sound the Latin makes but not the meaning.

EH But those are cases of possession—magical possession.

MH A form of colonization, I would call it.

EH An appropriation, yes. You seem more and more to have a distinct theoretical position, which I am grateful to learn about. Have you written about it?

MH Well, I wouldn't call it a theoretical position. Originally it was a practical position which I later, occasionally, theorized about. I have written some short pieces on translating and I've done lectures on the subject, since I was asked about it. Then, of course, I had to ask myself what I was doing. Oh yes, in the introduction to the last of my Hölderlin translations I did go into these questions a bit. That was after Lowell's *Imitations* had been published and I was a bit needled by the things he said there concerning other kinds of translators who don't do imitations, especially when he talks about taxidermists—I think he calls them that. ... Well, so I was a bit needled by some of Lowell's provocative remarks, but they made me think about what I had been doing. In another case, George Steiner had edited a Penguin book of poetry in translation in which he said that all the younger translators he included had translated in the manner of Ezra Pound. I wrote Steiner a note saying, "I don't translate in the manner of Ezra Pound, and so what you're saying isn't accurate." He said, "Well, you came after Pound, so you must translate in his manner."

EH   That's a bit sticky, isn't it?

MH   Then I became more and more aware that my practice was not that of most poet-translators who are at work now.

EH   Have you read Steiner's book, *After Babel*?

MH   No, I have not.

EH   Something else along that line, then: I am reminded of Carne-Ross's recent criticism of Robert Fitzgerald's translation of the *Odyssey*; Fitzgerald is scored for lacking the kind of primitive strength one looks for in Homer. Though he respects Fitzgerald, Carne-Ross says that Christopher Logue's translations of Homer—and Logue is a man who evidently knows much less Greek than Fitzgerald—are superior, at least in their forcefulness. What do you think of the criticism?

MH   Well, I don't know. I find it very hard to judge. It could well be that in ten years, say, the Fitzgerald version will still be read because the kind of language Logue has used would already be dated, because he uses a lot of contemporary slang and that sort of thing dates like anything. I suppose that may only mean that all such things have to be done over and over every ten years or so.

EH   I was thinking that Carne-Ross, who is an academic rather than a poet, appears to prefer the *un*academic translation, and that seemed curious.

MH   That's so because he knows the original and is not actually looking for a version that will help him read the original or be a substitute for it, but something that will give him the kind of thrill comparable to the one you get after reading it in the original. I suppose needs are quite different. There, of course, the different ways of translating also relate to the different reasons why people use and read translations. I think that the person who doesn't know the original at all or only knows it a bit must want something that gives some idea of what the original is actually like, and therefore a completely free imitation is of no use. Therefore, for example—this is obviously true—people don't read Pound's "Homage to Sextus Propertius" to learn what Propertius is like, but because they like Pound. The same applies to Lowell's imitations. These really are different things, aren't they?

EH The use a translation gets determines one way of evaluating it since there's no absolute criterion about translation. Would you agree?

MH No, I don't think so. You have to grant from the start that there are different types of translation and they all have a use and a value. That doesn't mean that all translations are equally good. There are bad translations in all the categories, including free imitations. You get a lot of very bad poetry passed off as an imitation of this or that.

EH I've heard someone say—I think it was Willard Trask—that when it comes to learning about an ancient author he prefers going to the Loeb Library edition where you at least can find something close to an interlinear trot, so that you know precisely what the original is *like*.

MH I think that person is probably mistaken because the linear trot doesn't actually give him anything of the poetry at all. In fact, he would have to make up the poetry for himself as he goes along. It does tell him more or less what is being said and that is what makes the whole thing so difficult.

EH There's such a variety of uses of translation—as much, I suppose, as of poetic forms themselves. Well, are there some thoughts on translation you have not expressed—I mean in the brief time we have left, before you have to go?

MH Well, I would like to say that I agree with what you said—or maybe you were quoting someone else—was it Willard Trask in another context? All translation is impossible and *that* is the reason why one does it. I agree with that entirely. In fact, I have said the same thing myself.

EH   That makes translation into a heroic and a foolhardy act at the same time.

MH   Well, I think all the things that are worth doing are impossible. Only impossible things are worth trying to do.

EH   Good. Then we have a lot to do. Thank you.

11 / Christopher Middleton

EH I'd like to begin by asking what started you as a translator, if you can recall when you began.

CM I was in Zurich teaching English at the University of Zurich and writing my Ph.D. I found a poem by Gottfried Keller that I thought I would translate just to see what would come of it. (Which is more or less what I've been doing in translating poems ever since.) On second thought, though, it occurs to me that I translated something before that. When I was a student at Oxford, I translated a poem by Walther von der Vogelweide, at the request of Peter Russell for his magazine *Nine*. That was a very formal poem, in rhymed quatrains. But it wasn't the formality of the poem that attracted me. It was some other quality of the language—an immediately luminous quality. I wanted to see if something of this luminosity could be invented in English.

EH So you don't remember translating poetry before the invitation of Peter Russell?

CM No, no.

EH By that time, however, you did know German quite well.

CM Yes, but then as now it's a question of meeting resistance. My German isn't perfect. I'm not bilingual. There is usually in a text I want to translate some kind of resistance; my work is to find out what that resistance is made of, or how I can grapple with it—this is the stimulus that I need. . . . I mean, something I don't understand, which I feel is worth understanding.

183

EH   German is the main language you've translated out of—is that true?

CM   Yes. Well, when I was a schoolboy I learned Greek and Latin and some French. I used to be quite good at Latin. I can remember very clearly when I was twelve I discovered that quite suddenly I could construe Latin sentences, and even write them. It was very exciting. During that early craze for learning, I also tried my hand at cuneiform and hieroglyphics—and Hebrew. Learning was mysteries, language kept them intact too. I was never good at languages; but the sense of mystery stayed with me. I was reading Merejkowski's novel about Leonardo. I also remember a time when I discovered the purity of Greek vowels. It was beside an English country stream, I was convalescing from an illness. Soon after that I did my first translation—I'd clean forgotten—it was from Horace. I didn't even start learning German until 1945. So it came late. By that time I was nineteen. I was taught German in order to become an interpreter in the Air Force, and I went to Germany. But mostly as a student I was reading German and not speaking it. I learned to write too, doing dull classroom translations. But it is a language that I came to relatively late, and to which I find my *Sprachgefühl* much more attuned than it is, for instance, to French, which I still have great difficulty in speaking or writing, unless I get loosened up, as by living in France a few months, after which I feel all right about it. But I find it very difficult to translate from French because it has for me a less accessible system of signs and sounds.

EH   So German is a language you've gotten to know, originally and at least partly, as a necessity—the business related to the war and then the literary challenge.

CM   Yes.

EH   When you did the medieval translation, and later again in Zurich, did you think of the activity as something you wanted to be involved in for a length of time—for instance, that you wanted to translate *a* poet?

CM   No. I never felt that. It was just a particular text that caught my attention for some reason. I never thought of translating anything long and I never thought of dedicating my energies to the translation of the whole works of an author. It was very sporadic, amateurish, dilettante, very ad hoc.

EH   Has it remained that way?

CM Yes. In those days, incidentally, I would invariably opt for a text that appealed to me but that would have no conceivable appeal for a publisher. I never really had publication in mind. And for many years it was like that. I suppose I had been translating five, or six, perhaps seven years before any possibility of publication arose. No, that's not quite accurate. In Zurich I translated a long text—a seventy-page story by Robert Walser, a Swiss-German author whom I more or less discovered, thanks to a student, while I was there. And I sat down and translated seventy pages in a few days. A very strange kind of fiction. That was published actually in 1957 by John Calder, with a subvention from a Swiss cultural foundation. But it was quite some time until Grove Press took *Modern German Poetry*.

EH I see. You say you were put onto Walser by a student. But I don't understand fully what the instigation was.

CM Well, the student showed me a book of Walser's, and I immediately felt, here was a kindred spirit, someone whose language was utterly unlike any other German I had ever read and whose mental agility I found congenial and admirable. It *suited* me. And I felt that I could mimic his agility in English.

EH Had you felt that before—in translating von der Vogelweide?

CM No, it was much more difficult before, mimicking the formality of von der Vogelweide's strophic forms. The rhymes were tiresome in English; they came out rather bookish, strained. But I think that in all these cases, whenever I have translated, it has always been to some extent a question of mimicry—of feeling a way patiently and persistently into the mentality of the author without necessarily going behind or beyond the text.

EH How many of your translations have been published?

CM The only things I have translated that haven't been published are seventeen essays by Rudolf Kassner and a book of memoirs about modern artists by Hans Richter, which I did at his request.

EH Richter the movie maker?

CM Yes, and he could not find a publisher for the book: *Encounters with Artists*—from his early days in Zurich right through to the present, from Tzara and Duchamp to Calder and Beuys.

EH You don't seem to distinguish between prose and poetry, at least as far as your personal inclinations are concerned.

CM Well, to be quite straight about that—most of the prose I've translated has been commissioned, whereas a great deal of the poetry has been
instigated by myself, and for my own interest.

EH So with the poetry it's a matter of pleasure over necessity.

CM To some extent, yes. But luckily, having a profession, I haven't
often had to translate. Even when I am commissioned, and it's not just
for the money, the text itself has to be of interest.

EH Do you have an attitude about the translation, either developed
from your own practice or from that and other points of view? Something that gives you a sense of what a good translation is, or how a good
translation is evolved?

CM I have no theory. The thing is, I don't like theorizing about it,
pressed as one is to theorize about literature when one is teaching. Translation is for me an intimate, secret, and intuitive activity, and I've never
risked thinking out how I do it or why I do it. I'd rather it be a spontaneous, unconscious, nontheoretical thing. On the other hand, I would
agree that the translators are there to put themselves at the service of the
spirit of the author. I have thought about this a good deal, on two counts:
one is that most of the imitations I have seen I haven't liked, and it seems
to me either a false way of translating or a false way of doing your own
work. On the other count, I wouldn't like it myself if a translator wanted
to translate something that I'd written in English, and then didn't do in
his own language what I had spent so much energy and trouble doing in
my own. I wouldn't like to see him, for instance, using my text as a pre-
text for going off in his own direction.

EH So you don't feel that imitations are a good idea. Lowell's "imitations," for example?

CM I don't like Lowell's "imitations," though I suppose that there
might be such things as great imitations, and that there is an area where
imitation and translation overlap. I'm thinking of Aldington's translation
of *The Golden Ass* and of Chapman's Homer. It may depend upon how remote in time the language of the original text is. Example: Arrowsmith's
version of Aristophanes' *Birds*, which is both imitation and translation.
But I think the imitation of a text that belongs, more or less, to one's own
cultural epoch is a different thing from an imitative reconstruction of an
ancient text. I prefer an ingenious and living translation to one that devi-
ates from the original, which is what an imitation usually does.

EH Well, we alluded to this the other day when I was talking to your translation class: whether one preferred, say, Christopher Logue's Homer to Robert Fitzgerald's, Logue's being the "imitation" and Fitzgerald's the careful transposition.

CM It depends what you're looking for. If you want an exciting text to read, you make your choice. But if you need to feel confident that what you're getting is close to the real Homer, it's obvious which one you'd choose. The real Homer?—"Who dat?" On the other hand Logue's Homerian extract, helped by Donald Carne-Ross, and involving, incidentally, some stylistic exercises of his own, which are Brechtian rather than Homeric—I must say that when I first read it I was alerted to all sorts of possibilities in the English language and all sorts of realities of Greek sensibility that I'd not felt very strongly before. It was a very exciting experience. And it's not Cecil B. DeMille's ancient Rome. I felt it was going to the core of the kind of shining, subtle and supple, muscular Greek sensibility of Archilocus or of Euripides—anytime during that span.

EH But then you actually respect the ability to incarnate a strong sense of the original, of the raw business itself, if that's the word. You want a translation that is not just literary but which goes deep into the sound and root of the original.

CM Yes, yes.

EH Is it possible to speak of that kind of thing—the qualities, say, that are important to render in translation? Let's take your own experience.

CM It would be very difficult to enumerate those qualities. It is necessary to know as much as you can about the whole work of the author. Not necessarily about his life or epoch, but to be receptive to the stratagems of his mind, his kind of sentence, and the kind of syntactical behavior his language shows. It would be useful to have this anyway, so as to keep one from failing to serve him on hitting a difficult incoherent patch, when one can only guess what he's really doing there; that is, you guess intelligently rather than wildly. I think that becoming receptive to a particular text and the ways in which one shows one is receptive, are things it's better not to speak about. Speaking about them upsets the balance of the elements in some strange kind of way.

When I was translating Georg Trakl, for instance, I didn't want to talk about it with anybody. I knew some of the other Trakl translations, and I had thought to talk with Michael Hamburger about the whole enterprise before launching into it. But even to talk to myself about how I was feeling, how I was responding, was to bring things to a level of consciousness that was likely to falsify.

EH   There's an element of wanting to hold the thing very close to your chest.

CM   Yes.

EH   Do you think this has anything to do with some unfinished thing, like the relationship-in-progress between you and the author you're translating? It's a relationship that is not really confirmed until you finish the translation.

CM   Yes. If then.

EH   There's an element also perhaps of wanting to keep it to yourself for fear of its leaking away otherwise, I mean by showing it to others.

CM   Yes, I feel the same thing, you know, in my own work. I don't like to talk about it when I'm doing it—that spoils it. It's got to be nourished somehow in the unconscious, in the preverbal; sheltered, I suppose, in a womb. And with translations—which are mediated rather than *im*mediate creations—it's the same. That's why, also, I never like to consult another translation of the text that I'm working on until I finish it, or to consult a friend as to how he would interpret, say, an ambiguous word, until I am so far along with my own translation that I can entrust it to the manifest world. You see, one mothers one's creations in a rather strange way.

EH   Well, that would rule out having an informant—at least until you'd finished your version.

CM   Yes, yes. For this reason too, I've never been able to translate from a language I don't know, and so to need an informant—though I have risked it once or twice, I never got any pleasure, never felt I was really doing anything.

EH   You mentioned earlier having other languages besides German. Actually you haven't translated from French, say.

CM   No, not much. Some poems, mainly, some prose by Tsepeneag, too, but I don't trust myself with French. I don't know it well enough and I can't initiate it myself, whereas I can initiate German.

EH   As someone who also teaches and sees students grappling with

texts and perhaps their own poems, do you consider translation to be
a good didactic exercise?

CM   Theoretically, it's fine for students to do, yes. You can learn a lot
from translation, and about your own language too. But I know it's very
tiresome when the teacher has to take home twenty muddled, bad, and
ultimately incorrigible translations every week and correct them. It's
a very tiresome sort of teaching. I did that for ten years in London, every
week.

EH   Let me ask you something now about the German poet Hölderlin.
He seems to be crucial, perhaps, for anyone interested in German
poetry. As say Wordsworth would be in English, and Whitman in
American poetry.

CM   Yes.

EH   I know that Michael Hamburger has spent many years of his life
translating Hölderlin. And one hears more and more about him now.
You've done some work on Hölderlin too.

CM   Yes, I translated about thirty poems for a book that I rashly undertook to do for Chicago University Press.[27] I selected Hölderlin and
Mörike as poets I wanted to translate but didn't know if I could. I particularly wanted to do Mörike because the particular translations that I'd
glanced at seemed to me to be bookish, and they hadn't gotten anywhere
near the freshness and the nerviness of his very subtle idiom. And I
wanted to translate Hölderlin because I felt that Michael Hamburger's
pioneering and exemplary translations hadn't touched a certain quality
of Hölderlin's language. Michael had done explicative translations. He
made Hölderlin, I felt, less turbulent, less doubting, less troubled, in
some ways. Because that's what Michael was there to do: he was opening
Hölderlin up to speakers of a completely different language in a completely different epoch. But I felt that something else could be done.
I wanted to see if I could do it.

EH   You chose the particular poems, then.

CM   Yes.

EH   And did you do it?

CM   Yes, I did it. I don't know with what success. What I tried to do
there was a very difficult thing, and this was to be a bilingual edition
designed to be of use to students in universities. Well, I wanted to make

a translation that would be quite faithful, in the conventional sense, but that at the same time had distinct poetic qualities matching those in Hölderlin, and that would make people want to read him. There may already be students walking around who have actually felt the power, whose very flesh has trembled, right there in the classroom. I hope so. Yet I wanted also to provide them with a "reliable" Hölderlin version.

EH   Line for line.

CM   Yes, pretty well—except for some of the later, supposedly fragmentary, poems, where I rearranged the lines to accord with a more Poundian or Olsonian format.

EH   And you chose the poems from all parts of his work?

CM   Except that I omitted his very early poems. They begin about 1798, when he was already in his maturity, and go right through to 1805 or whatever. Many of these poems are in formal, classical measures and in strophic forms, such as Alcaic and Asclepiadic, also elegiac distichs. I'd never written anything of my own in these forms, and I wanted, again, to see if this could be done in a vital way in English. In that case, as in all translating of poetry, you've got to extend your own linguistic resources beyond their normal limits so that you reach out with both hands and touch the original. You've definitely got to modify, modulate, and transfigure your own linguistic resources—and extend them. What you're really doing is exploring new possibilities.

EH   So your doing translation was a job of testing and challenging your skills as an English poet as well as establishing an equivalent in English for students wishing to compare it with the original. Was there any contradiction here between freedom and necessity?

CM   Well, if the truth consists of contradictions, I would hope that that would be the case. Evidently, the student whose German is minimal would be helped by following my translation; then he would perceive his own original as his capabilities developed. He might even go so far as to discover that the way I translated is not the way he would have translated. And so perhaps a new translator would have been born. On the other hand, I must say that I didn't feel any contradiction while I was at work on the translations, and that's the way I've always tried to translate poetry—in terms of service to the letter of the original text, the word as something ultimate, despite the provisional nature of all language—and at the same time the translation as a poem in its own right: the kind of poem the author would have written if he had been writing in my language. I think my sympathies were with Josef Brodsky when he lambasted certain translators of Mandelstam in the *New York Review of Books* some time ago. Those translators, to his thinking, had scorned the incarnate word—which is what Mandelstam's poems are about. Perhaps Brodsky went, or goes, too far. There are Russian rhymes—how could any translator reconstitute the whole body of Mandelstam's sound? But I'm still a purist, rather than a slap-happy approximator. Haroldo de Campos said to me: "Unless the something is too difficult to translate, it's not worth translating." *Jabberwocky*, translated by Haroldo and his brother into Portuguese, is a case in point.

EH   Do you think that in the case of Hölderlin, now after—what is it?—thirty years since Michael began to translate him, that he's more available in a variety of ways which makes it possible to assimilate him, difficult and strange poet that he is, into English? Do you think that process has developed?

CM   Yes, of course, but then Hölderlin has been on the scholarly map for a long time, and I would rather hope that translations of Hölderlin, as they appear, would make him less and less accessible, so that he can't be assimilated, so that he retains his ferocity, doesn't get tamed, doesn't get what the French call *récupéré*.

EH   My view is something of this sort: the way in which English poets took over the surrealists and perhaps also the wild boys, Rimbaud and Lautréamont, around say the 1930s, was a way of recharging the juices of English poetry. Perhaps the phrase is not "assimilating the poets" but using them to advantage, so that the existence of very good translated texts would be of great service to a literary movement—the literary sensibility wanting to create something different in English. Assimilating in that sense, then.

CM   Yes, the effect is to enable you to look over the edges of the conventions of your own language. Some poets, in England especially, seem most reluctant to do this. There is a hostility to anything they call "foreign," in that pursed-lip middle-class English way of speaking. On the other hand, I've always been in search of "the other," in so many different sectors of life. It may be I translate as a compulsive pursuit of "the other," which at other times can take other forms. I don't mean this in a metaphysical way; but I do think that growth comes through encounters with the alien, the foreign, the strange, and the unknown. And one of the simplest and most creative ways of considering the act of translation is to regard it as a minimal, perhaps vestigial, but still exemplary encounter with "the other." And the translator who imitates is getting to know "the other"; on the other hand, the translator who writes an imitation is ignoring the autonomous reality of "the other" because he's just reducing that text to his own preestablished terms.

EH   That's a very good point, I think. You put it very well. And to make it clear now: the objection to an imitation that doesn't go beyond the resources of the poet-translator is that he's not discovering anything new. I wonder if this doesn't suggest that you give something away as well as try to do a service or you throw something out of yourself. Or as we say, there's a great *risk* involved.

CM   Yes, that's true. One can overtranslate. What we were talking about earlier in the day comes into it. Fornicators get bored with making love.

EH   The translating Don Juans.

CM   Translators who go on translating all the time just can't stop doing it. They do anything that comes before them. The Don Juan translators—or transfornicators, whatever they are—are perhaps not going to develop or retain a unique capacity for writing their own things. On the other hand, there may be people who decide along the line: O.K., I'm not really there to be an originator; I'm doing better work as a humble copier. They're not fornicators, they're just humble servants of the word.

EH   Do you see such people—you may have some particular ones in mind, perhaps—as able to evolve a style or to imitate the style, say, of a German poet? Or does it take a person like yourself, that is, another poet, who has already found a distinctive style of his own, to know what a style is? I'm not sure it's a question that's fair to ask. It's rather hypothetical.

CM   I think the test case would be a man like Pound, with a very distinctive metric and phonology; when he translates something, it's Pound. Wilbur doesn't dominate Molière in that way, nor does Edmund Keeley dominate Seferis. Let's say: there are constructor-translators like Pound and receptor-translators like Keeley. And one shouldn't expect either to be the other. I like to be a constructor when I write my own things; when I'm translating I like to be a receptor or a transformer: you receive and transform the current as it comes into you and it goes out in another direction, though perhaps not at the same wattage.

EH You mention Keeley, and I have spoken with him. As you are aware, he has almost always translated with a collaborator, Philip Sherrard, a Greek scholar with a special field in Byzantine history. And Mike Keeley himself is a novelist. So their collaboration seems rather unusual.

CM Yes, they're monkish, I'd say. Without having taken any particular vow, they're under a vow of humility, because they're not setting themselves up as poets on someone else's basis. They're serving the word of Seferis and of Cavafy. And they've done a tremendous service for people who can't read Greek. But God forbid that Seferis should ever be translated by Ezra Pound, because then no one would know Seferis.

EH Now, can we talk a moment about your piece on Franz Mon:[28] a close case study of a translation you'd done of a sort of concrete poem?

CM Not really a concrete poem, but an experimental, continuous text rather too wordy to be concrete. Mon has been associated with concrete poets, but this is a very difficult, exploratory, subliminal, fractured kind of text.

EH I think you said that you began to understand the poem only after you'd translated it.

CM Yes.

EH Is this a usual experience? Or would you ordinarily want to know what it was about before starting?

CM No, sometimes there's just a bit of phrasing in a poem that catches my attention, and then I translate some Mon. It was for an anthology I was editing. As I went on with the text, I became aware more and more of how much I didn't understand. Translating it was bringing me first to a recognition of that fact; and then, when I was thinking about the problems I was having in translating it, I very slowly began to understand the poem.

EH Did you get to like the poem in the process of translating it?

CM I began to get to like my idea of it as a structure that is partly fragmented and also partly intact syntactically. So I began to see the relationship between the fragmented and the unfragmented parts.

EH It's not a dramatic poem, though there's a definite voice in it. You say about it that you saw a relationship between Mon's procedure and that of the Cabalists of the Middle Ages. Something about the sacred relationship between the letters and the plotting in them of mystic truths. Would that imply there was a voice in the Mon poem like that of a mystic seer?

CM No. It does a great deal with sound but it's an oddly nonvocal poem. You don't hear a distinctive voice but you can hear sounds, almost without the presence of vocal cords.

EH How then would it be read?

CM I think it would be murmured. It's a kind of murmuring ruminant poem. Many more poems than one thinks are precisely that. You know, when you go to poetry readings you're used to hearing poems spoken in loud and clear voices, but many of those poems really should be murmured.

EH Are you prepared to read this poem in German? Perhaps some part of it.

CM I could have a go at it. [*Starts reading, with the initial word* "*Grundriss.*"] The last three lines are a quotation from a folk song.

EH They made me think of the lines, "Alle Menschen werden Brüder." The repetition there seemed like the swelling of a chorus.

CM The odd thing in that poem is that Mon has sounds without tonality, sounds without vocal cords that are in part optically recognizable, in part auditory. It isn't a poem in which you have to listen to resonances and timbre.

EH Does the poem interest you from that point of view—I mean as a possible way of writing yourself?

CM Not really. I find it rather cerebral and arid, it's not got much blood in it.

EH You said earlier that translation was a very engrossing and overwhelming experience and that you don't like to keep going back to it.

CM I don't like to do it too much because when I'm translating a poem—or any text actually—I pursue this "other" obsessively and compulsively, and I can't think or do anything else. That's why, when I've been asked to do a longer prose work, I've been very reluctant to undertake the job. The two novels I've translated are both short, and the critical work I've translated—Canetti's book on Kafka's correspondence with Felice Bauer—was only about 110 pages. I can translate a 250-page book in three weeks, if it's in prose. But usually I start pretty slowly and have to work maniacally during the last week—about fifteen or sixteen hours a day. And it is an incubus.

EH   By that time you've gotten into it, and you can't get out.

CM   Yes.

EH   Then, do you go over it? Of course you must.

CM   I hate going over it again, but I do. Yes, I go over it very carefully, and I usually hope, too, that a sensible, well-informed editor will guide me, and pick up slips I might have made.

EH   Were those novels you did contemporary?

CM   Near enough. One was a contemporary East German novel by Christa Wolf, which I did in three weeks when I was in Vienna, including the typing, incidentally. And the other was an older novel, by Robert Walser, published first, I think, in 1909.

EH   Then you've had the experience of doing novels from two different periods. I mentioned to you that Michael Hamburger finds novels harder to translate than poetry.

CM   Yes, because of the dialogue and idiomatic phrasing. Well, there isn't much dialogue in the Walser novel. In the Wolf novel there is a good deal, but it's strangely neutral. It's not stylized in the way that Hemingway's is, or Laurence Sterne's, or even Stendhal's. I didn't find it difficult to do because I felt the characters were speaking a straight old-fashioned, stuffy East German German. To make it into believable, living English speech, I had to switch the word order quite a bit, bring it around and make it sound right.

EH   Were there any particular problems?

CM   Yes, it's a curious novel about East Germany, also Berlin. But I don't know if I really want to talk about it.

EH   Well, O.K. Now, my last question is, again, a hypothetical one. My observation of W. S. Merwin as translator and poet is that he does both jobs very well. But there may be a hidden threat involved when one does as much translation as he has done—at least to one's own work. Often I can't tell the difference between his translated and his original work. Not, however, from the usual point of view, but rather from an impression that his own spirit as poet has disappeared into the thing he's translated. One gets the same disembodied voice in everything he does.

CM   Yes, that's true.

EH   Do you think there's a danger in overextending oneself as a translator?

CM   Yes, I think so. The crux is the mysterious phenomenon of rhythm. And Bill Merwin's is an interesting case. I don't think he has a distinctive rhythm, which may facilitate his work as a translator. He can mimic the rhythms of the poets he's translating, because there are none of his own that get in the way. I think this holds for Pound too, but otherwise Pound's unmistakable measure tends to enter into whatever he does—whether he's translating from Chinese or from Latin, and I'm thinking of his "Cathay" as well as his "Propertius." If a poet has discovered his own rhythm in all possible modulations, he won't be writing poems as if they were translated from another language. But even then rhythm is something precarious and delicate, and you might just lose your rhythm or your touch, if you assimilated rhythms from so many poets in other languages. They disperse your own.

EH   I don't know what the mechanism of Merwin's verse might be that gives me this impression. Whether my impression of it is true or not is another question. Still, you tend to agree, don't you?

CM   Yes, I do.

EH   But that it concerns rhythm hadn't occurred to me.

CM   Yes, rhythm is the mysterious nature of being—biological or intellectual. This is such a difficult thing to talk about. But rhythm is surely something fundamental to the origin and maintenance of life—whether it's physical or verbal life. Some people talk about being, talk about the cosmos, or "the other," the universal language, or the language of the universe, and the rest of it. . . . The common denominator of all these concepts is rhythm. The difficulty of course is that that's a reductive kind of argument. If you ask me what rhythm is, I could probably not tell you, although I would say there are rhythms, and all artists have to discover their own rhythms or they never realize themselves, they never activate all their resources. I suppose that what we do is attempt to modulate a deep rhythm, which of its own nature cannot really be manifested or enacted; yet all poets, all translators approximate it.

EH   I like that. You're coming closer to my metaphysical idea, in some way, of the "absent text."

CM   I'm quite—I wouldn't say convinced, but I can quite confidently entertain the fiction of "the absent text" because I think that there are un-utterable truths, that certain mysteries resist language, or that one cannot speak of certain things. Reading Octavio's [Paz] remarks about this—in that published conversation you showed me—which I find very noble, convincing, I would argue the other way around and say that the only conceivable *Ur*text or absent text is the one we are helped to conceive of by the existence of the text before us. And, in my logic, that is to deny the preexistence of an *Ur*text. The *Ur*text can only be the imaginary construct that we can obtain *post rem*, the *rem* being the text as it is. It cannot be something metaphysical that preexists or is *ante rem*.

EH   Nobody has seen the face of God, though the Bible says He created us in His own image.

Afterword

The sense of the particularity of words, with which the translator begins, may well relate to an earlier and deeper fascination with the physicality of voice producing the sound of words. The ritualized tonalities associated with alien-sounding languages or bits of foreign language, even though meaningless, often stay with the child forever. One begins to see that the word-cum-voice, as spoken on and with the tongue, is locked inside a sound, a rhythm, an intonation and, like any body gesture, takes on a sensual life of its own. The infant recognizes its mother, as the married man his wife, by a single syllable of her voice, which the hearer immediately translates into *mother* or *wife*. Similarly in the poem, the poet's words start with the speaking voice intoning, seeking to make words accurately reflect the sounds that only the poet's voice can make, unique as a thumbprint. Imitating the words, gestural sounds associated with the quality of himself loving and hating, he searches for the qualities, the echoes of these things in engaging himself to another. Through love he appropriates words, through hate, dispels or denies them. He imitates and translates in order to transmute them for his own use. Once the words are merged with him he can forget them, at least not have to recall them consciously again; he may even come to discard them as no longer him.

I suppose a tacit recognition of such phenomena underlay these conversations. In some sense the conversation itself as dialogue, as symposium, conducted near the writer's table, desk, or fireplace, seemed to celebrate the common mysteries, acts, and voicings called *translation*. Our interest in each other's practice and techniques invariably focused on the incandescent approach to the transformative process, the variety and spread of personal style. As conveyor and purveyor of such pryings and elucidations, I wanted to represent the mosaic of many eyes and hands at work, the many personae engaged in producing the translations. Taken all together, the conversations resolve themselves into something like a graph of the conditions under which translation is possible.

When I asked how they got started translating, some fraternal or parental figure invariably showed up at the source. Ben Belitt's was a close friend, the critic Wallace Fowlie, who started him on the French symbolists, although he went off on his own later to become the translator of Lorca and Neruda. Wilbur began at Harvard by putting into English some poems of André du Bouchet, a fellow graduate student, who in turn put Wilbur's poems into French. "Knowing André," he says, "I was able to begin the translation of any one of his poems with a sense that I knew his tones of voice and preoccupations." For Trask in Paris after World War I, it was George Marguliès: "a Russian who had the gift for languages raised to the point of genius," with whom he "collaborated on some translations from the Chinese. We also found that we were interested in the same things. We were both reading the French Renaissance poets, and he said, 'Well, you must learn Spanish because you'll love Lope de Vega.' So I learned Spanish."

For most translators the rule seems to be that a warm encouraging other voice at the start facilitates the transforming of the foreign idiom into their own. Also pressing them is the immanent voice of the original, begging to be recast. As Renan had put it, "une oeuvre non traduite n'est publiée qu'à demi." Some translators who work with informants experience the reassurance of a living figure who sometimes proves to be, as with Keeley, the original poet himself. Knowing the language fluently, the mentor appears responsibly adult, a father who takes you by the hand to the zoo—the zoo of another language.

Octavio Paz's experiment with the *renga* involved a group of like-minded poets, each in a different language creating one poem together.

When I observed that this brings together the translation and the original in one act, Paz replied that all translation is typically a transformation, the living presence of absent voices. "We were only the instruments of *another* author. This author was the language itself—the language that was also changing as we wrote, changing with the tongue of each poet." Translation discovers the text's other voice, its significant expressibility, not the mechanical transmissibility of content simply to serve the reader. In this way it also leads the poet to discover his other voice. Discovering other voices is essential, since without them translation would be impossible. "Translation as an art begins" where voice engages the "materiality of the signs, its physical properties" waiting to be transformed. For "since you cannot use the same signs of the original, you must find equivalents. The text is lost but its effects can be reproduced through other signs; with different means, but playing a similar role, you can produce similar results. I say *similar*, not *identical*. Translation is an art of analogy, the art of finding correspondences. An art of shadows and echoes."

For Belitt similarly, the art of transforming one voice into another is crucial. "I would say translation is neither a solitary voice nor a collective voice. It is an attempt to express one's own exuberance or one's own sense of contact with things." This being so, he says, "I myself don't know how to separate my own voice from the initiating voices because the initiating voices furnish a continuing motive for my own."

Fitzgerald and Wilbur variously seem less inclined to stress the particular influence of initiating voices and to try more for a transformation of Homer or Molière on their own terms. Their stated aim of "equivalent thought" implies proceeding according to the line-by-line mandate of the text rather than by way of analogy. Keeley, Hamburger, and Middleton, if not Trask and Hollander, appear to opt for equivalent thought as a guiding principle. As for Trask, who was the only participant to favor the principle of transposition—"a translation should sound like a translation," giving it the savor of the original language from which it was made—the role of translator, like that of actor, stand-in, or musician, is largely interpretive.

Although for Mason, too, the only translation that makes sense is interpretive, unlike Trask he believes himself to be an intermediary hearing a voice beyond the personal which invokes his personal talents. But since his subject is the *Gilgamesh*, an oral epic, the point must be qualified when he adds "to pretend to have a true text is to miss the point of the whole process of oral narration," since the translator must not only be an imitator and an interpreter but an in-the-flesh actor as well.

Another voice-mode of being or becoming turns Fitzgerald into an epic poet via Homer or Vergil, and Wilbur into a dramatist-using-couplets via Molière. Thus their insistence on the stability of the text implies a modus operandi in translating. For Paz, on the other hand, there cannot be a single text. "There is always an *Ur*text—the never written and never spoken 'original,' always virtual and always appearing in many versions, all saying the same thing and saying different things." For the postsymbolist who takes language to be a microcosmos, the double of the universe, and therefore transformational, a stable text cannot exist. The translation that re-creates a poem changes it by necessity, as one civilization changes another by adapting and consummating its uses. Part of the same mandate—to complete the preexistent—is felt by Richard Wilbur. "Don't we often," he observes, "well before the 'idea' of a poem has begun to clarify, feel an odd certainty about the proportions of what is coming on, about its tenor, savor, stance, or mode—about the channels of logic or feeling in which it is going to run?" And he refers to Mallarmé's "awakening of a voice, perhaps his own, 'Encore dans les plies jaunes de la pensée. . . .' What I mean is that the subject, before we fully know it, seems often to have done a good deal of occult marshaling."

Associating the existence of the text with the transformative process it must undergo, I have elsewhere noted that the phenomenon resembles "a shadow or a projection [of the foreign poem] on the photographic plate, say, of one's own language. The space between words is actually where the poem exists rather than in the words. One first arrives at a prose sense of the poem . . . then one has an illumination about what lies between the prose version and the original. One should have that illumination with every poem one translates; otherwise the poem won't get off the page."[29]

Does the transforming effort also make for a change in the data? Frederic Will, the poet-translator, suggests that this process must involve "a transition from *being taken hold of by something*, some force or being, or some element of notself, without any personal effort on the part of the poet, to *an active taking hold of something by the poet*—a producing, an animating or reanimating of something within himself, which only his personal effort can make available to him. The content of his poetry changes from something that is 'given' to something that has to be grasped or achieved."[30]

For Christopher Middleton, a clear distinction must exist between the materiality of the text and the translator's effect on it. "I can confidently entertain the fiction of 'the absent text' because I think there are unutterable truths, that certain mysteries resist language, or that one cannot speak of certain things. Reading Octavio's remarks about this . . . which I find very noble, convincing, I would argue the other way around and say that the only conceivable *Ur*text or absent text is the one we are helped to conceive of by the existence of the text before us. And, in my logic, that is to deny the preexistence of an *Ur*text. The *Ur*text can only be the imaginary construct that we can obtain *post rem*, the *rem* being the text as it is. It cannot be something metaphysical that preexists or is *ante rem*."

Answering this sober and revealing statement, my remark, "Nobody has seen the face of God, though the Bible says He created us in His own image," may seem facetious. But I am grateful for Middleton's instigating statement because it provides the context in which the remark may begin to be seriously entertained.

One comes around in the end to where one began, with the inherently dynamic functions and yearning of language toward change. What is it one translates? Many translations fail because the translator is readily disabled by following a false notion of fidelity to the original instead of being faithful to his own total view of its imaginative import. Confirming such a view is William Blake's famous dictum that "all had originally one language and one religion." Accordingly, each act of translation is an attempt to heal the division and restore the unity of all languages to the condition of man before he committed the third act of pride—the building of the Tower of Babel. It is only where all is a transforming act fully engaging the imaginative faculty that the translation merges with the original.

Notes

1. "On Translating Calderón," *Michigan Quarterly Review* 11, no. 4 (1972): 264–71.

2. Robert M. Adams, *Proteus: His Lies, His Truth* (New York, 1973).

3. John Hollander, "Versions, Interpretations, and Performances," in *On Translation*, ed. Reuben A. Brower (Cambridge, Mass., 1959), pp. 205–31.

4. Adams, *Proteus*.

5. Frederic Will, *The Knife in the Stone: Essays in Literary Theory* (The Hague, 1973).

6. Irving Howe and Eliezer Greenberg, eds., *A Treasury of Yiddish Poetry* (New York, 1969).

7. "The Golem," trans. John Hollander, in Jorge Luis Borges, *Selected Poems 1923–1967*, ed. N. T. di Giovanni (New York, 1972), pp. 111–15.

8. Adams, *Proteus*.

9. George Steiner, *After Babel: Aspects of Language and Translation* (New York, 1975).

10. Herbert Mason, *Gilgamesh: A Verse Narrative* (New York, 1970).

11. *Salmagundi* and *Review '74*. See also Ben Belitt, *Adam's Dream: A Preface to Translation* (New York, 1978), where these pieces are reprinted.

12. Guy Daniels, "The Tyranny of Free Translation," *Translation 73* 1, no. 1 (1973): 12–20.

13. *The Learned Ladies* (see Biobibliography).

14. Wilbur subsequently translated Molière's *School for Wives* as well as Racine's *Andromaque* (see Biobibliography).

15. Richard Wilbur, "Authors on Translation," *Translation 74* 2, no. 7–8 (1974).

16. On this comment Professor Levin himself observes: "That is roughly true but slightly misleading, since it gave me the privilege of a belated induction by Milman Parry, who went over my part with me very carefully, line for line and word for word."

17. George Seferis, *The King of Asine and Other Poems*, trans. N. Valaoritis (London, 1948).

18. Edmund Keeley, "T. S. Eliot and the Poetry of George Seferis," *Comparative Literature* 8 (Summer 1956): 214–26.

19. *The Poems of C. P. Cavafy* (New York, 1952).

20. George Seferis, *Collected Poems, 1924–1955* (Princeton, 1967).

21. *George Seferis: Poems* (Boston, 1961).

22. Edmund Keeley, "On Translating Cavafy and Seferis," *Shenandoah* 23 (Winter 1972): 39–49. Col. under the title "Problems in Rendering Modern Greek," in *Essays in Memory of Basil Laourda* (Thessaloniki, 1975).

23. Edmund Keeley's remarks about Cavafy in the context of this conversation antedate his book, *Cavafy's Alexandria* (Cambridge, Mass., 1976). The more elaborate discussion of these matters must of course be sought there.

24. "Seferis' Elpenor: A Man of No Fortune," *Kenyon Review* 28, no. 3 (1966).

25. Keeley, "On Translating Cavafy and Seferis."

26. Pierre Loving, *Short Poems by Friedrich Hölderlin* (Girard, Kansas), 1925.

27. *Selected Poems of Friedrich Hölderlin and Eduard Mörike* (Chicago, 1972).

28. Christopher Middleton, "On Translating a Text by Franz Mon," *Delos* 1, no. 1 (1968): 67–79.

29. Henry James Cargas, "The Translator, the Poet: An Interview with Edwin Honig," *Webster Review* 3, no. 4 (Fall 1977): 11.

30. Will, *Knife in the Stone*.

Biobibliographies

Ben Belitt

Ben Belitt, born in New York City in 1911, has only "institutional and hermetic" memories of his first ten years spent in a large public orphanage. He considers his real birth to date from the early 1920s, after his mother remarried and took him to live in a large frame house in Lynchburg, Virginia. It was for the teachers of the high school there that he wrote his first poems and stories, influenced by Poe and "the world of the impossible." He took both his B.A. (1932) and his M.A. (1934) at the University of Virginia, but abandoned work on a doctoral dissertation when an editor offered him an assistantship at the *Nation*, where he worked from 1936 to 1937. Belitt has taught at Bennington College since 1938. He served in the United States Army during World War II (1943–44).

AWARDS AND HONORS: Shelley Memorial Award for Poetry (1936); Guggenheim Fellowship (1946); *Quarterly Review of Literature* Fiction Prize (1950); Oscar Blumenthal Award in Poetry (1956); Chicago Civic Arts Award (1957); Brandeis Creative Arts Award in Poetry (1962); National Institute of Arts and Letters Award in Poetry (1965); National Endowment for the Arts grantee (1967–68); Russell Loines award for Poetry, American Academy and Institute of Arts and Letters (1981).

POETRY: *The Five-Fold Mesh*, 1938; *Wilderness Stair*, 1955; *The Enemy of Joy: New and Selected Poems*, 1964; *Nowhere but Light: Poems, 1964–69*, 1970; *The Double Witness: Poems, 1970–1976*, 1977.

PROSE: *Adam's Dream: A Preface to Translation* (essays), 1978.

TRANSLATION: *Four Poems by Rimbaud: The Problem of Translation*, 1947; Federico García Lorca, *Poet in New York*, 1955; *Selected Poems of Pablo Neruda*, 1961; Antonio Machado, *Juan de Mairena and Poems from the Apocryphal Songbooks*, 1963; *The Selected Poems of Rafael Alberti*, 1965; Jorge Guillén, *Cántico* (with others), 1965; Eugenio Montale, *Selected Poems* (with others), 1966; *Neruda: A New Decade: Poems 1958–67* (with Alastair Reid), 1969; Pablo Neruda, *Poems from the Canto General*, 1969; Rafael Alberti, *Poems to Painting*, 1972; Neruda, *Splendor and Death of Joaquín Murieta*, 1972; Neruda, *New Poems: 1968–70*, 1972; *Jorge Luis Borges: Selected Poems (1923–67* (with others), 1972; Neruda, *Five Decades: Poems 1925–70*, 1974; Neruda, *Skytones*, 1981; Lorca, *Earth and Moon*, 1982; Lorca, *The New York Poems*, 1983.

Robert Fitzgerald

Robert Fitzgerald was born in 1910 in Geneva, New York, but spent his early years in Springfield, Illinois. He studied philosophy and classics at Trinity College, Cambridge, and returned to the United States to get his B.A. at Harvard in 1933. Fitzgerald later worked as a journalist for the *New York Herald Tribune*. He published his first book of poems in 1935; the next year his translation (with Dudley Fitts) of Euripides' *Alcestis* was issued. He then began writing for *Time* magazine, and subsequently became editor of the book section. After military service with the Navy, he returned to writing book reviews for *Time* and to teaching at Sarah Lawrence College. He also wrote poetry reviews for the *New Republic*. When Fitzgerald received his first Guggenheim Fellowship in 1953, he moved with his family to Italy. In 1957 he returned to the United States and subsequently taught at Notre Dame, the University of Washington, and Mount Holyoke College. From 1965 until his recent retirement he was Boylston Professor at Harvard University; he died in January 1985.

AWARDS AND HONORS: Guggenheim Fellow (1953, 1972); Shelley Award, Poetry Society of America (1956); National Institute of Arts and Letters award (1957); Grant for Creative Writing, Ford Foundation (1959); Bollingen Prize for Translation (1961); Landon Award for Translation (1976); Ingram Merrill Literary award (1978).

POETRY: *Poems*, 1935; *A Wreath for the Sea*, 1943; *In the Rose of Time*, 1956; *Spring Shade*, 1972.

TRANSLATION: Euripides, *Alcestis* (with Dudley Fitts), 1936; Sophocles, *Antigone* (with Fitts), 1939; Sophocles, *Oedipus at Colonus*, 1941; Sophocles,

Oedipus Rex (with Fitts), 1949; St. John Perse, *Chronique*, 1960; Homer, *Odyssey*, 1961; Perse, *Birds*, 1966; Homer, *Iliad*, 1974; Vergil, *Aeneid*, 1983.

EDITIONS: *The Collected Poems of James Agee*, 1968; *The Collected Short Prose of James Agee*, 1968; Flannery O'Connor, *Mystery and Manners* (with Sally Fitzgerald), 1969.

Michael Hamburger

Michael Hamburger, the son of a medical specialist and professor of medicine, was born in Berlin in 1924. He emigrated with his family in 1933 to Britain, where he felt "something of a freak" because of his early German background. At sixteen, he knew he wanted to be a writer, and while doing his own work, he began translating J. C. F. Hölderlin. The translation of German authors has since become a central focus of Hamburger's career: through "both inner and outer pressures," Germany has remained "his constant and primal concern." Hamburger spent four years in military service during World War II (in Britain, Italy, and Austria)—a time that was "at once formative and disruptive of any sort of unified personality." After the war, he attended Oxford University, where he received his M.A. in 1948. He later took jobs in England as lecturer in German at the University College, London (1952) and the University of Reading, where he taught until 1964. Subsequent teaching positions in the United States have taken him to Mount Holyoke, SUNY at Buffalo and at Stony Brook, and Wesleyan University. For his sixtieth birthday, Carcanet Press published Hamburger's *Collected Poems* in the spring of 1984.

AWARDS AND HONORS: Bollingen Foundation fellowship awards (1959, 1965); Award of the Cultural Committee of German Industrialists for translation from German (1963); Deutsche Akademie für Sprache und Dichtung (1964); Translation Prize—Arts Council of Great Britain (1967); British Arts Council Prize (1969); Levinson Prize (1970); Schlegel-Tieck Prize (1978, 1981); Wilhelm-Heinse Prize (1978).

POETRY: *Flowering Cactus*, 1950; *Poems, 1950–51*, 1952; *The Dual Site*, 1958; *Weather and Season*, 1963; *In Flashlight*, 1966; *Feeding the Chickadees*, 1968; *Travelling*, 1969; *Travelling, I–V*, 1973; *Ownerless Earth*, 1973; *Travelling VI*, 1975; *Real Estate*, 1977; *Moralities*, 1977; *Variations*, 1981; *Collected Poems*, 1984.

PROSE: *Reason and Energy* (critical essays), 1957; *Hugo von Hofmannsthal: Zwei Studien* (criticism), 1964; *From Prophecy to Exorcism: The Premises of Modern German Literature* (criticism), 1965; *Zwischen den Sprachen: Essays und Gedichte* (essays and poems), 1966; *The Truth of Poetry* (criticism), 1969; *Contraries* (criticism), 1970;

Hofmannsthal: Three Essays (criticism), 1971; *Art and Second Nature* (criticism), 1975; *A Proliferation of Prophets* (essays), 1984.

TRANSLATION: J. C. F. Hölderlin, *Poems of Hölderlin*, 1943 (revised as *Hölderlin: Poems*, 1952); Charles Baudelaire, *Twenty Prose Poems*, 1946; Ludwig van Beethoven, *Letters, Journals and Conversations*, 1951; Georg Trakl, *Decline*, 1952; Albrecht Goes, *The Burnt Offering*, 1956; Hölderlin, *Selected Verse*, 1961; Hugo von Hofmannsthal, *Poems and Verse Plays* (with others), 1961; Bertolt Brecht, *Tales from the Calendar*, 1961; *Modern German Poetry 1910–1960* (edited with Christopher Middleton), 1962; von Hofmannsthal, *Selected Plays and Libretti* (with others), 1964; Georg Büchner, *Lenz*, 1966; H. M. Enzensberger, *Poems*, 1966; Günther Grass, *Selected Poems* (with Middleton), 1966; Hölderlin, *Poems and Fragments*, 1967 (new enlarged edition, 1980); Enzensberger, *The Poems of Hans Magnus Enzensberger* (with Jerome Rothenberg and the author), 1968; Enzensberger, *Poems for People Who Don't Read Poems*, 1968; Grass, *The Poems of Günther Grass* (with Middleton), 1969; Peter Bichsel, *And Really Frau Blum Would Very Much Like to Meet the Milkman*, 1968; Günther Eich, *Journeys*, 1968; Nellie Sachs, *Selected Poems*, 1968; Bichsel, *Stories for Children*, 1971; Paul Celan, *Selected Poems*, 1972 (new enlarged edition, 1980); *Peter Huchel: Selected Poems*, 1974; *German Poetry 1910–1975*, 1977; *Helmut Heissenbüttel: Texts*, 1977; *Franco Fortini: Poems*, 1978; *An Unofficial Rilke*, 1981.

ANTHOLOGIES AND EDITIONS: *East German Poetry: An Anthology*, 1972; *German Poetry, Nineteen Ten to Nineteen Seventy-Five*, 1977; *German Literature from Nietzsche to the Present Day*, 1983.

Max Hayward

Max Hayward was born in London in 1925 and died on March 18, 1979. As a youth he accompanied his father, an itinerant worker, traveling from place to place throughout England. His early interest in gypsies led to his buying a book about them in Russian, and, in order to read it, he taught himself the language. Subsequently he received his formal education at Oxford University. He was editor of the *London Daily Telegraph* and, later, adviser to Harvill Press, Chekhov Press, and Harcourt Brace. Employed by the British Embassy in Moscow, Hayward witnessed Stalin's purge of artists, writers, and the intellectual community. Thereafter he devoted himself to preserving many banned works of dissident Soviet authors. As translator he was responsible for bringing to the attention of the West the major works of Russian authors, including Boris Pasternak, Aleksander Solzhenitsyn, and Andrei Sinyavsky.

AWARDS AND HONORS: Oxford University Fellow; Harvard University Fellow.

PROSE: *The Ideological Consequences of October, 1956*, 1957.

TRANSLATION: Boris Pasternak, *Doctor Zhivago* (with Manya Harari), 1958; Vladimir Mayakovsky, *The Bedbug and Selected Poetry* (with George Reavey), 1961; Aleksander Solzhenitsyn, *One Day in the Life of Ivan Denisovich* (with Ronald Hingley), 1963; Andrei Sinyavsky, *Fantastic Stories* (with Hingley), 1963; Solzhenitsyn, *For the Good of the Cause*, 1964; Izak Babel, *You Must Know Everything*, 1969; Nadezhda Mandelstam, *Hope Against Hope*, 1970; Andrei Amalrik, *Involuntary Journey to Siberia* (with Harari), 1970; Anna Akhmatova, *Poems* (with Stanley Kunitz), 1973; Mandelstam, *Hope Abandoned*, 1974; Eugenia Ginzburg, *Journey into the Whirlwind* (with Paul Stevenson), 1975; Olga Ivanskaya, *A Captive of Time*, 1978; Abram Tertz, *A Voice from the Chorus* (with Dyril Fitzlyon), 1978.

ANTHOLOGIES AND EDITIONS: *Dissonant Voices in Soviet Literature* (with Patricia Blake), 1964; *Halfway to the Moon: New Writing from Russia* (with Blake), 1964; *On Trial: The Soviet State Versus "Abram Tertz" and "Nikolai Arzhak"* (with Leopold Labedz and Harari), 1966; Andrei Voznesensky, *Antiworlds and the Fifth Ace*, 1967; *Religion and the Soviet State*, 1969; Aleksander Gladkov, *Meeting With Pasternak: A Memoir*, 1977; Voznesensky, *Nostalgia for the Present* (with Vera Dunham), 1978; *Soviet Russian Literature*, 1983.

ADAPTATION: *The Telephone* (with William Jay Smith, fiction adapted from the Russian text *Telefon*, by Kornei Chukovsky), 1977.

John Hollander

John Hollander, born in 1929 in New York City, came from a family of Eastern European and German Jews who provided "a home that buzzed with ideals and enlightenment." At sixteen, Hollander attended Columbia University, where Mark van Doren and Lionel Trilling were his teachers and Allen Ginsberg, a friend and critic. He studied English literature and art history, receiving his B.A. in 1950. After a period of traveling and working in Europe (where one of his jobs was to write program notes for classical record liners), Hollander returned to the United States to do graduate work at Columbia (M.A., 1952) and Indiana University (Ph.D., 1959). While a Junior Fellow in the Society of Fellows at Harvard, he lived in Cambridge, playing early music and studying the history of music in preparation for his doctoral dissertation, *The Untuning of the Sky: Ideas of*

Music in English Poetry, 1500–1700 (published in 1961). His first collection of poetry, *A Crackling of Thorns*, won the Yale Younger Poets Award (1958). Hollander has taught at Connecticut College, Hunter College (CUNY), and Yale, where he has been since 1977.

AWARDS AND HONORS: Yale Younger Poets Award (1958); Poetry Chap Book Award (1962); grantee of the National Institute of Arts and Letters (1963); Levinson Prize (1964); Overseas Fellow at Churchill College, Cambridge University (1967–68); Senior Fellow, National Endowment for the Humanities (1973); Guggenheim Fellow (1979); Bollingen Prize (1983).

POETRY: *A Crackling of Thorns*, 1958; *Movie-Going, and Other Poems*, 1962; *A Book of Various Owls*, 1963; *Visions from the Ramble*, 1965; *Types of Shape*, 1968; *The Night Mirror*, 1971; *Selected Poems*, 1972; *Town and Country Matters: Erotica and Satirica*, 1972; *The Head of the Bed*, 1974; *Tales Told by the Fathers*, 1975; *Reflections on Espionage*, 1976; *In Place: A Sequence*, 1978; *Spectral Emanations: New and Selected Poems*, 1978; *Blue Wine and Other Poems*, 1979; *Powers of Thirteen*, 1983.

PROSE: *The Untuning of the Sky: Ideas of Music in English Poetry, 1500–1700*, 1961; *The Quest of the Gole*, 1966; *Vision and Resonance: Two Senses of Poetic Form*, 1975; *The Figure of Echo: A Mode of Allusion in Milton and After*, 1981; *Rhyme's Reason: A Guide to English Verse*, 1981.

ANTHOLOGIES AND EDITIONS: *Poems of Ben Jonson*, 1961; *The Wind and the Rain* (with Harold Bloom), 1961; *Jiggery-Pokery* (with Anthony Hecht), 1966; *Poems of Our Moment*, 1968; *Modern Poetry: Essays in Criticism*, 1968; *American Short Stories since 1945*, 1968; *The Oxford Anthology of English Literature* (with Frank Kermode), 1973; *For I. A. Richards: Essays in His Honor* (with R. A. Brower and Helen Vendler), 1973; *Literature as Experience* (with Irving Howe and David Bromwich), 1979.

Edmund Keeley

Edmund Keeley, the son of a career diplomat, was born in 1928 in Damascus, Syria. When he was three the family moved to Canada, then to Greece where Keeley lived from ages eight to eleven. He came to the United States in 1939 and went to high school in Washington, D.C. After graduating from Princeton in 1950, Keeley taught under the Fulbright program at the American Farm School in Salonika. At Oxford, where he completed his D.Phil. in 1952, he met and married Mary Stathatos-Kyris, a Greek woman who has since collaborated with him on translation. They return every summer to a plot of land near Limni, Euboaea. Until recently, most of Keeley's own writing has been centered on his strong Greek associations. After finishing his D.Phil., he returned to the faculty at Princeton University, where he is head of the Creative Writing Program. Principally a novelist, Keeley has also been deeply engaged in translating modern Greek poetry with two collaborators—Philip Sherrard and George Savidis.

AWARDS AND HONORS: Prix de Rome Fellowship of the American Academy of Arts and Letters (1956–57); Guggenheim Fellowship (1956–57); Guinness Poetry Award (1962); Columbia University Translation Center-PEN Translation Award (1975); National Endowment for the Arts Creative Writing Fellowship (1981–82); Howard T. Behrman Award for Distinguished Achievement in the Humanities (1982).

PROSE (NOVELS): *The Libation*, 1958; *The Gold-Hatted Lover*, 1961; *The Imposter*, 1970; *Voyage to a Dark Island*, 1972.

TRANSLATION: *Six Poets of Modern Greece* (with Philip Sherrard), 1960; Vassilis Vassilikos, *The Plant, The Well, The Angel* (with Mary Keeley), 1964; *Four Greek Poets* (with Sherrard), 1966; George Seferis, *Collected Poems 1924–55* (with Sherrard), 1967; Constantin Cavafy, *Selected Poems* (with Sherrard), 1972; Cavafy, *Passions and Ancient Days: 21 New Poems* (with George Savidis), 1972; *Modern Greek Writers* (with Peter Bien), 1972; Cavafy, *Selected Poems* (with Sherrard), 1972; Odysseus Elytis, *The Axion Esti* (with Savidis), 1974; Cavafy, *Collected Poems* (with Sherrard and Savidis), 1975; Angelos Sikelianos, *Selected Poems* (with Sherrard), 1980; *The Dark Crystal: Poems by Cavafy, Sikelianos, Seferis, Elytis, Gatsos* (with Sherrard), 1981; Elytis, *Selected Poems* (with Sherrard), 1981; *Yannis Ritsos: Return and Other Poems, 1967–72*, 1983.

Herbert Mason

Herbert Mason was born in Wilmington, Delaware, in 1932. He received his B.A. (1955), M.A. (1965), and Ph.D. (1969) from Harvard University. Mason worked in a variety of fields before becoming an author, educator, and translator. Besides involvement in summer theater and work as a schooner crewman, he played semiprofessional baseball in 1950, and in 1954–55 was employed as a private detective. Mason has taught at Wentworth Institute (1950–57), American School of Paris (1959–60), St. Joseph's College (1960–62), Simmons College in Boston (1962–63), Tufts University (1966–67), and Harvard University (1964–68). He also worked as a translator on a series project for the Bollingen

Foundation from 1968–72 and was co-editor of *Humaniora Islamica* in 1973 and
1974. Since 1972 Mason has been a professor of religion and Islamic history at
Boston University.

AWARDS AND HONORS: Kittredge Fellowship (1957); National Book Award
Nomination (1971).

POETRY: *Gilgamesh: A Verse Narrative* (adaptation), 1971; *The Death of al-Hallaj*,
1979.

PROSE: *Reflections on the Middle East Crisis*, 1970; *Two Statesmen of Medieval Islam*,
1971; *Moments in Passage*, 1979; *Summer Light* (novel), 1980.

TRANSLATION: Louis Massignon, *The Passion of Al-Hallaj*, 1981.

Christopher Middleton

Christopher Middleton was born in 1926 in Truro, Cornwall, where his father
was a professor of music and organist of the cathedral. In 1930 his family moved
to Cambridge, and from the age of ten he attended boarding schools in idyllic,
country places. This "sheltered musical and scholastic background" was something Middleton would later violently rebel against. During World War II he
served as RAF aircraftman-interpreter. After the war, Middleton went to Merton
College, Oxford University, to study German and French; he received his
D.Phil. in 1954. Middleton has been a lecturer in English at the University of
Zurich and, in the ten years following, taught at King's College, University of
London (1955–66). Since 1966, he has been professor of Germanic languages at
the University of Texas at Austin.

AWARDS AND HONORS: Sir Geoffrey Faber Poetry Prize (1963); National
Translation Center grantee (1966–67, 1969–70); Guggenheim Fellowship for
Poetry (1974–75); Guest Writer of German Academic Exchange Artists Program
in Berlin (1975, 1978); Poetry Fellowship from the National Endowment for the
Arts (1980).

POETRY: *Poems*, 1944; *Nocturne in Eden*, 1945; *Torse 3: Poems, 1949–1961*, 1962;
The Metropolitans (comic opera, music by Hans Vogt), 1964; *Nonsequences/
Selfpoems*, 1965; *Der Taschenelefant*, 1969; *Our Flowers and Nice Bones*, 1969; *The Fossil
Fish*, 1970; *Wie wir Grossmutter zum Markt bringen*, 1970; *Briefcase History*, 1972;
The Lonely Suppers of W. V. Balloon, 1975; *Pataxanadu & Other Prose*, 1977;
Carminalenia, 1980; *Woden Dog*, 1982; *111 Poems*, 1983.

PROSE: *The Pursuit of the Kingfisher: Essays*, 1983.

TRANSLATION: Robert Walser, *The Walk and Other Stories*, 1957; Gottfried Benn, *Primal Vision*, 1960; Hugo von Hofmannsthal, *Poems and Verse Plays* (with others), 1961; *Modern German Poetry* (edited with Michael Hamburger), 1962; Günther Grass, *Selected Poems* (with Hamburger), 1966; Georg Trakl, *Selected Poems* (with others), 1968; *Selected Letters of Friedrich Nietzsche*, 1969; Grass, *The Poems of Günther Grass* (with Hamburger), 1969; Walser, *Jakob von Gunten*, 1970; Christa Wolf, *The Quest for Christa T.*, 1970; *Selected Poems of Friedrich Hölderlin and Eduard Mörike*, 1972; Elias Canetti, *Kafka's Other Trial*, 1974; Walser, *Selected Stories*, 1982; Goethe, *Selected Poems*, 1983; Christoph Meekel, *The Figure on the Boundary Line: Selected Prose*, 1983; Gert Hofmann, *The Spectacle at the Tower*, 1984.

ANTHOLOGIES: *No Hatred and No Flag, 20th-Century War Poems*, 1958 (published in German as *Ohne Hass und Fahne*, 1959); *The Poet's Vocations: Selections from the Letters of Hölderlin, Rimbaud, and Hart Crane* (edited with William Burford), 1962; *German Writing Today*, 1967.

Octavio Paz

Octavio Paz was born in 1914 and grew up on the outskirts of Mexico City. At seventeen he founded the avant-garde review *Barandel*, and at nineteen he published his first book of poetry, *Luna silvestre*. At the outbreak of the Spanish Civil War (1936), Paz left for Spain to enlist in the Republican cause. While there he was befriended by numerous Spanish and Latin American poets, among them Federico García Lorca, Pablo Neruda, Vicente Aleixandre, and Miguel Hernández. On his return to Mexico City, he founded and edited the literary reviews *Taller* (1939) and *El Hijo Pródigo* (1943). In 1945 he entered the Mexican diplomatic service, which took him during the next few decades to Paris, where he met André Breton, Jean-Paul Sartre, Albert Camus, and Jules Supervielle, and to Japan and India, where he immersed himself in the Buddhist and Taoist classics, Oriental painting, poetry, and architecture. In 1968 he resigned his ambassadorial post in India in protest over Mexico's brutal repression of students in Tlatelolco. Paz subsequently taught at Cambridge University, the University of Texas (Austin), the University of Pittsburgh, and Harvard University. He now lives in Mexico City, where he edits the Mexican monthly *Vuelta*.

AWARDS AND HONORS: International Poetry Grand Prix (1963); National Prize for Literature (Mexico, 1977); Jerusalem Prize (1977); Critics Prize (Spain,

1977); Golden Eagle Prize (France, 1978); Ollin Yoliztli Prize (Mexico, 1980); Cervantes Prize (Spain, 1982); Neustadt International Prize for Literature (1982).

POETRY: *Luna silvestre*, 1933; *Raíz del hombre*, 1937; *Bajo tu clara sombra y otras poemas sobre España*, 1937; *Entre la piedra y la flor*, 1941; *A la orilla del mundo*, 1942; *Libertad bajo palabra*, 1949; *Águila o sol?*, 1951; *Semillas para un himno*, 1954; *Piedra de sol*, 1957; *La estación violenta*, 1958; *Agua y viento*, 1959; *Libertad bajo palabra: obra poética, 1935–57*, 1960; *Salamandra*, 1962; *Vrindaban, Madurai*, 1965; *Viento entero*, 1965; *Blanco*, 1967; *Discos visuales*, 1968; *Ladera Este*, 1969; *La Centena*, 1969; *Topoemas*, 1971; *Renga* (with Jacques Roubaud, Eduardo Sanguineti, and Charles Tomlinson), 1972; *Pasado en claro*, 1975; *Vuelta*, 1976; *Poemas 1935–75*, 1979; *Tiempo nublado*, 1983.

POETRY IN ENGLISH TRANSLATION: *Sun Stone* (Piedra de sol), 1957; *Selected Poems, 1953–57*, 1963; *Eagle or Sun?* (Águila o sol?), 1970; *Configuration*, 1971; *Renga: A Chain of Poems*, 1972; *Early Poems, 1935–1955*, 1973; *A Draft of Shadows and Other Poems*, 1979; *Selected Poems*, 1984.

PROSE: *El laberinto de la soledad*, 1950; *El arco y la lira*, 1950; *Las peras del olmo*, 1957; *Cuadrivio*, 1965; *Los signos en rotación*, 1965; *Puertas al campo*, 1966; *Corriente alterna*, 1967; *Claude Lévi-Strauss o el nuevo festín de Esopo*, 1967; *Marcel Duchamp o el castillo de la pureza*, 1968; *Conjunciones y disyunciones*, 1969; *Postdata*, 1970; *El mono gramático*, 1971; *Las cosas en su sitio*, 1971; *Traducción: literatura y literalidad*, 1971; *El signo y el garabato*, 1973; *Los hijos del limo*, 1974; *Marcel Duchamp: apariencia desnuda*, 1978; *Xavier Villaurrutia en persona y en obra*, 1978; *El ogro filantrópico*, 1979; *In/ mediaciones*, 1979; *La busqueda del comienzo*, 1980; *Rufino Tamayo*, 1982; *Sor Juana Ines de la Cruz o las trampas de la fe*, 1982; *Sombras de obras: arte y literatura*, 1983; *Poesia en movimiento*, 1983.

PROSE IN ENGLISH TRANSLATION: *Labyrinth of solitude* (El laberinto de la soledad), 1961; *Claude Lévi-Strauss: An Introduction* (Claude Lévi-Strauss o el nuevo festín de Esopo), 1970; *Marcel Duchamp or the Castle of Purity* (Marcel Duchamp o el castillo de la pureza), 1970; *The Other Mexico: Critique of the Pyramid* (Postdata), 1972; *The Bow and the Lyre* (El arco y la lira), 1973; *Alternating Current* (Corriente alterna), 1973; *Conjunctions and Disjunctions* (Conjunciones y disyunciones), 1973; *Children of the Mire* (Los hijos del limo), 1974; *The Monkey Grammarian* (El mono gramático), 1981; *Marcel Duchamp: Appearance Stripped Bare* (Marcel Duchamp: apariencia desnuda), 1981; *On Poets*, 1983; *Rufino Tamayo: Myth and Magic* (Rufino Tamayo), 1983.

TRANSLATION: Fernando Pessoa, *Antología*, 1962; William Carlos Williams, *Veinte Poemas*, 1973; *Versiones y diversiones*, 1974.

Willard Trask

Willard Trask, the son of American parents, was born in 1900 in Berlin and died on August 10, 1980, in New York City. Because his father was an engineer who traveled widely, Trask lived in Germany, France, Russia, England, and Panama before the age of ten. He attended Harvard University, but dropped out and moved to France to study medieval poetry. Returning to the United States during the Depression, Trask supported himself "by odd jobs in the sewers of literature" until an editor suggested he try translation. Thereafter he translated works from Spanish, French, Portuguese, German, Italian, Chinese, Finnish, Catalan, and Wendish. Although Trask spent a lifetime translating, he is best known for his acclaimed translation of Giacomo Casanova's twelve-volume *The History of My Life*, from an unexpurgated French manuscript released from a German publisher's vault after World War II.

AWARDS AND HONORS: National Book Award, 1967; Gold Medal, Translation Center of Columbia University, 1978.

TRANSLATION: Ramón José Sender, *Chronicle of Dawn* (prose), 1944; Yves Simon, *Community of the Free* (prose), 1947; Zoé Oldenbourg, *The World Is Not Enough* (novel), 1948; Victor Serge, *The Case of Comrade Tulayev* (prose), 1950; Johann Scheffler, *The Cherubinic Wanderer* (poetry), 1953; Erich Auerbach, *Mimesis: The Representation of Reality in Western Literature* (prose), 1953; José Ortega y Gasset, *Man and People* (prose), 1957; Sainte Jeanne d'Arc, *Joan of Arc: Self-Portrait* (prose), 1961; Friedrich Hölderlin, *Hyperion; or The Hermit in Greece* (poetry), 1965; Giacomo Casanova, *The History of My Life* (prose), 1966; Benjamin Franklin, *The Bagatelles from Passy* (prose), 1967; *The Unwritten Song* (poetry), 1967; *A Treasury of the World's Finest Folk Songs* (collected and arranged by Leonhard Deutsch), 1967; *Medieval Lyrics of Europe* (poetry), 1969; Mircea Eliade, *Zalmoxis the Vanishing God* (prose), 1972; Georges Simenon, *The Hatter's Phantoms* (novel), 1976.

Richard Wilbur

Richard Wilbur, the son of an artist, was born in New York City in 1921 and spent his early years in New Jersey "in one corner" of a country estate. He admits that his rather solitary boyhood in the midst of this pastoral setting had a strong influence on his later poetry. At Amherst College, Wilbur interested himself in journalism and spent summers touring most of the United States by freight car until 1942, when he married. It was not until World War II that he began seriously to write poetry, his first collection appearing in 1947. Wilbur received a B.A. degree from Amherst College (1942) and an M.A. from Harvard University

(1947). After his graduate studies, he became a member of the Society of Fellows at Harvard for three years. Wilbur has taught in English departments at Harvard, Wellesley, and Wesleyan; he is poet in residence at Smith College and lives in Cummington, Massachusetts, in a large country house.

AWARDS AND HONORS: Harriet Monroe, Oscar Blumenthal Prizes from *Poetry* magazine (1948, 1950); Guggenheim Fellowship (1952–53); Prix de Rome Fellowship of the American Academy of Arts and Letters (1954); Edna St. Vincent Millay Memorial Award (1957); National Book Award (1957); Pulitzer Prize (1957); Ford Foundation Fellowship (1960); Bollingen Prize (1971); Harriet Monroe Poetry Award (1978); PEN Translation Prize (1983); Drama Desk Award (1983); St. Botolph's Club Foundation Award (1983).

POETRY: *The Beautiful Changes*, 1947; *Ceremony, and Other Poems*, 1950; *A Bestiary*, 1955; *Things of This World*, 1956; *Poems 1943–56*, 1957; *Candide: A Comic Operetta* (libretto with Lillian Hellman and others), 1957; *Advice to a Prophet*, 1961; *Poems of Richard Wilbur*, 1963; *Walking to Sleep: New Poems and Translations*, 1969; *Opposites* (children's poems), 1973; *The Mind-Reader*, 1976; *Seven Poems*, 1981.

PROSE: *Loudmouse* (children's prose and poems), 1963; *Responses: Prose Pieces, 1952–1976*, 1976.

TRANSLATION: Molière [Jean Baptiste Poquelin], *The Misanthrope*, 1955; Molière, *Tartuffe*, 1963; Molière, *The School for Wives*, 1971; Molière, *The Learned Ladies*, 1978; *Molière: Four Comedies*, 1982; Jean Racine, *Andromache*, 1982; *The Whale* (uncollected translations), 1982.